Praise for the book

It's great to see that we have such books coming out especially from young biz wizards like Adit, as they would definitely bring in a new perspective to New Age marketing.

Praseed Prasad, *Head of Media, Flipkart*

Marketing: Tricks of the trade they won't teach you at B-schools, will hit you with its simplicity and practical approach just as marketing should. The core KRAs of marketing as a function are manifested in the form of each of its chapters in a sequential and logical way to the extent that one could achieve excellence in marketing by ensuring a focus on each of them and evaluating the progress periodically. Thankfully, Adit's writing is down to earth and has an approach that is granular but not boring.

Hemant Arora, *Sr. Vice President, Times Network and Business Head, Times Influence*

As a management teacher and practitioner I can say that this book will be extremely resourceful and ingenious for management students, entrepreneurs and intrapreneurs. This book provides a valuable window on strategy-making and implementation at every stage of the business cycle. The specialty of the book is in its practical know-how of the marketing concepts and the discussions in it about things beyond the so-called marketing jargons. The examples are exceedingly straightforward and effortlessly palatable. This is an excellent guide for anyone who wants to understand marketing quickly but steadily.

Col. (Dr) Sneh V. Sharma, *Director, Amity Global Business School (Mumbai and Pune)*

Adit Chouhan has thought through what the current generation of marketers need and made this an interesting reading experience. In today's Google world, which is full of shortcuts and quick research, this one stands out as a legit and practical knowledge resource which is insightful and backed by his on-the-job learning. The chapters are comprehensive and well-defined. Each topic becomes a subject guide in itself. The book is highly recommended for students of marketing and all those who would like to consider a career in it. It will also act as a good refresher course for existing marketers. I would certainly call it a twenty-first century bible for marketing.

Sonia Kulkarni, *Senior Partner, Ketchum Sampark*

It's like a marketing handbook which every marketer should read. All your basics and nuances will be sorted once you read this book.

Ashish Gupta, *Vice President – Marketing, MobiKwik*

This is an interesting book on marketing. It communicates in a very clear and easy to understand manner. The author has succeeded in covering all aspects of media marketing from basics to details. A must-read for media and digital marketing enthusiasts, I highly recommend it!

Manish Jain, *Founder & CEO, Indus Business Academy, Bangalore and Director, MUHEPL, New Delhi*

This book is an easy read. It's like a one-day master class before you take your first job as a marketer. The fact that Adit Chouhan is not from academia actually works in favour for this book. His no-nonsense narrative style makes it appear as if he is sitting with you in a cafe and providing you with an insider's guide to do your marketing job.

Prasad Menon, *CEO, Centre for Incubation and Business Acceleration, Mumbai*

Adit's book tells you how to, in a contained, calm and systematic manner deal with marketing issues in real life. It tells you how to hit the floor running and be a real-life champ.

I congratulate him on this well-written book that lays out his thoughts in the most precise and systematic manner. A must-read for all marketing professionals, even those who went to the finest B-schools. Trust me, textbook theories make you an ostrich in a disaster but practical knowledge will turn you into a gutsy tiger.

Anshu Khanna, *Founder & MD, Goodword Media PR, New Delhi*

MARKETING

Adit Chouhan is a Marketing Coach, Digital Marketer, Entrepreneur and Writer. He has a B.E. in electronics and communications from VTU, Karnataka and is a postgraduate in marketing management from Symbiosis International University, Pune. His first start-up venture was Cornucopia Weekends Planner, and he has now founded CLICKS (www.clickstechnologies.com) – an effective and affordable digital marketing solutions agency, located in Pune. Chouhan has also recently started a first-of-its-kind lifestyle-based social commerce online platform called Style My Life (www.stylemylife.in). He lives with his wife in Pune, and enjoys teaching digital marketing to working professionals over the weekends. He can be reached at adit@aditchouhan.com

MARKETING

Tricks of the Trade They Won't Teach You at B-Schools!

ADIT CHOUHAN

RUPA

Published by
Rupa Publications India Pvt. Ltd 2017
7/16, Ansari Road, Daryaganj
New Delhi 110002

Sales centres:
Allahabad Bengaluru Chennai
Hyderabad Jaipur Kathmandu
Kolkata Mumbai

ISBN: 978-81-291-4808-7

First impression 2017

10 9 8 7 6 5 4 3 2 1

Printed at Parksons Graphics Pvt. Ltd, Mumbai

For

My parents (Mamma and Papa Hokam),
my sweet and sporty sister Neha,
and my wife Prerana, who always inspires me.

Contents

Preface

When I was doing my MBA in marketing from Symbiosis, Pune, I used to think that my course is making me more knowledgeable than a non-MBA out there working right after graduation, especially in the field of marketing. I bet it's the same thought that most of the B-school students have who are deeply involved in Kotler, the BCG matrix, the four layers of Brand Management, the 7Ps, and other marketing gyan!

However, reality strikes on the very first day of your job when you realize that what you studied was good theory but you would not be able to apply most of it to work. Instead, what you will need to do as a marketer will be lots of on-the-job learning to be able to excel in your field. A not-so-great introspection happens to you when you meet a non-MBA with much more hands-on practical knowledge of planning and execution than yourself. He seems more confident than you and that also hurts your ego as an MBA. And you think to yourself—*why was I not taught about all this practical matter during my two years of postgraduate studies?*

You will then try to come in the good books of some seniors and try to learn the tricks of the trade from them. This, in turn slows you down, slows your career growth, lowers your self-esteem, and puts you in the rat race. It forces you to follow the conventional path of learning on the job even after studying hard and clearing entrance exams to get through postgraduate courses.

The purpose of this book is to help you understand those things which ordinarily you will only learn on the job, after finishing your marketing course. However, I am no marketing legend. So, please do not have very high hopes here. But I have been through this journey during the early days of my, now ten-year-long, career. That's why I am sharing in this book some crucial tricks of the trade, which I learnt on my job too. And I can assure you that once you finish reading this book, you will be equipped with far superior and practical knowledge on marketing than any other theory book written till date. This book will be beneficial for:

1. Students of marketing.

2. Those pursuing a career in marketing.
3. Anyone trying to start a business or a freelance career in marketing.

Basically, it's for anyone interested or connected to marketing in any way.

So, if you are any of the above or close to it, the knowledge within the pages of this book will hopefully help you grow faster in your career and fulfil my purpose of preparing better marketers for the industry.

Hope you enjoy reading it as much as I have enjoyed writing it for you. Do visit www.aditchouhan.com to download/use more marketing support material and also to leave your comments.

Thank you!

Adit Chouhan

chapter one

What is Marketing?

Now, this is something that I am sure you already know. So, let's treat this section and the next few like a warm-up session so that you can get comfortable with my style of thinking and writing. Also, to make you feel that you are conversing with a friend and not reading a boring manual.

As I mentioned earlier, we are not going to discuss things in an extremely technical and unnecessarily theoretical manner here. We will look at things with a more practical approach. So, for me, the single, simple and coherent definition of marketing is:

> *The best possible way to reach out to your end consumer and influence him to make a purchase of your product or service.*

Let's break this definition into parts and dig a little deeper:

- **Best possible way**. There are multiple ways to reach out to your potential buyers but it is the duty of a marketer to continuously analyse his marketing activities and outcomes and find out the top three most cost-effective methods with highest reach and conversions to a purchase. You need to know what has worked for you the most.
- **Reach:** Your reach can happen through any of the senses like audio, visual, touch or smell depending on your innovation in marketing plans. However, the most important part to keep in mind is that your reach happens in the most impactful way possible for your product/service. For example: if you are selling incense then if you reach via newspaper distribution of a stick glued with the paper, it will be much more impactful than just a print or radio or outdoor ad with an image of the incense. Of course, these innovative campaigns cost more than regular advertising but the impact and brand recall is manifold.
- **Consumer:** You must know the difference between a Customer and a Consumer. A Customer is the one who purchases your product. Whereas, a Consumer is the one who finally uses your

product. A Customer is not always necessarily a Consumer. Best example of this are most of the products targeting kids. If you get a kid's attention, he will ensure that his parents buy your product. So, the parents are customers but the kid is your consumer.

- **Influence:** This is the tricky side of the whole marketing game! We all know that most marketing campaigns are way over the top. However, the most successful ones are those which can influence a person by means of knowledge sharing or emotional connect. Don't overpromise and always treat your consumer as an intelligent person to be able to influence their buying decision.
- **Purchase**: This simply means someone paying to buy whatever you are offering. However, in case your last mile is in the hands of a sales person then your work ends at the Lead Generation level itself. Converting that lead to a final purchase is in the hands of the sales person.
- **Product/Service**: This could be anything that comes under 'conversion' for you. If your marketing activity is focused towards people filling some forms and giving their details, then that's your achievement. If it is to ensure that people call on a certain number, then that's your achievement.

If its focus is towards increasing footfall in your store or property, then that is your achievement. So, the product/service definition varies as per the business.

Before beginning my postgraduation, I had similar knowledge of marketing as you might have without completing any professional course. Then I went through a two-year course with a lot of Kotler, the BCG Matrix, several case studies and what not. Only to realize that my academic knowledge is of no good in the real world at the start of my career. They did not expect me to sit in the strategy meetings and give gyan based on my academic excellence. It's basic field work and execution they expected me to do to understand the market first. Moreover, when I talked to any other colleague in the marketing department, even someone without an MBA, he/she seemed to have much more knowledge of the ground realities than I did. That was scary and will always be the same for you as well. Plus, this gives reasons to your seniors to treat you as if you don't know anything.

Yes, a professional course helps you understand the bigger picture quickly and helps you flaunt a few jargons here and there. But, the knowledge that you need to gain on-the-job at the start of your career or business is immense and not available in any professional course that I know of.

So, here we are, learning something much needed, together.

chapter two

Difference between Branding and Marketing

So, let's get the basics cleared first.

In the first glance, marketing and branding seem quite entangled and can be confused with one another. But, as you dig deeper, the differences between the two become much more clear than you can imagine.

Now, we have defined marketing earlier. It is the best possible way to reach out to your end consumer and influence him to purchase your product or service.

Branding, on the other hand, has nothing to do with this definition. Let's see how we can define a brand in layman's terms:

A 'brand' is the name you would like to be known as in your market, amongst your customers and your stakeholders.

There are companies which work intensively to suggest what your brand name should be. The process of deriving that name includes understanding your product/service offering, your company history, company philosophy, demographics of your potential customer/consumer and a lot of brainstorming.

For example: if the most important part of your company philosophy is trust, then the brand agency suggests a few colours, fonts, etc. reflecting that to the subconscious mind of a person. The brand design agency helps you also figure out whether your brand name and, hence, the logo needs straight edges or curves or both. There are a whole lot of technical as well as psychological points that are taken into account for finalizing a brand name and then coming out with a brand logo. The more detailed you are, the better it is for your brand.

The agency, once a brand name and logo are agreed upon, comes with a complete set of directions and rules for the brand treatment in a document called 'Brand Manual'. A brand manual will consist of dos and don'ts for your brand logo usage, colour palettes that can be used for the brand communication, and the other necessary brand guidelines.

Then, there is another detailed document that you receive from the brand design agency explaining how the store should look like, how the brand positioning should go on throughout the store to leave an impression on every customer that visits it.

Once you start executing all that is mentioned in these important documents created by a group of intelligent individuals specializing in brand design—that process, my friend, is known as 'Brand Creation'. It leaves a mark on a potential consumer's mind space. That is what branding is, as mentioned earlier.

However, if the information is not enough, please go ahead and google a bit about branding, brand design basics, brand communication and check a few brand design companies. You will definitely learn more about branding.

Of course, there are many more stages to a brand lifecycle and how you need to rethink and redesign your brand positioning to keep it fresh. But, we shall not get into those details here since that would take another book!

You will soon realize that most of the people you meet confuse branding with brand marketing opportunities. So, if your company logo is displayed as a presenter of a show/event or if your company presentation/AV is run during a show in front of the audience or your name is announced as a sponsor by an emcee few times during a show, then that's not branding. These are just brand marketing opportunities for 'Brand Recall'. Branding is what we have just covered in this section in a nutshell.

So, while a brand lifecycle is quite long and has no direct relation with the sales of product/service, marketing is the practice whose whole and sole purpose is to support the brand in achieving sales targets for the month, for the quarter and for the financial year.

Marketing could be tactical or strategic, could be combative (head-on, like the Coke–Pepsi war) or individual but it ultimately needs to show a Return on Marketing Investment (ROMI) and that's about it. Whatever you spend, you need to apply logic and calculate your expected ROMI before you spend. And keep a track of the same throughout the campaign.

That is broadly the difference between branding and marketing.

chapter three

What is a TG?

Let's be honest here. How many of us had heard of this jargon before entering a management course? I am not sure anyone has. Maybe a few did. What we didn't know is that this term will become the centre of our professional lives throughout!

TG = Target Group

This is where all our marketing efforts, our business, need to coincide. Our TG or Target Group. And how do you define this Target Group?

I believe, the whole economy of any system depends on the nature of supply and demand, and same is the case with any business. Any business first needs to identify if there is an existing demand for what it is offering. How big the demand is secondary at this stage. What matters is whether there is any demand at all or not.

If no, then business needs to re-think over its existence or if the demand can be created with evangelizing the concept and educating your customer. If yes, then you know you have a TG for your business and you need to dig deeper in that direction to crystallize your TG definition. In defining your TG, you will probably be answering the following questions:

1. Who wants to buy your product/service?
2. Why does he want to buy your product/service?
3. What will influence him to buy your product/service over your competition?
4. How much does he earn per month?
5. Are your customers mostly men or women, or both?
6. What is the character sketch of your potential customer? (Single/married, newly married/has kids, age, lifestyle, two-wheeler rider/four-wheeler rider, rented/own house, nuclear/joint family, etc.)
7. Geography of your potential customer—urban, tier-II/III, rural, location within a city, etc.

You can even add further specific questions as per your business.

Defining a TG helps you understand whether you are offering noodles (consumed by a rickshaw-driver also and perhaps by the rich too) or a Rolls Royce (meant only for a select few that too chosen by you). This eventually helps you identify various means to reach and influence your potential customer/ consumer.

And, that's what we will discuss in our next chapter.

chapter four

Media Vehicles (ATL and BTL)

We have discussed marketing. We have discussed branding. And, we have defined our TG.

Once we know who are we targeting, we need to know their life in the following manner, taken as an example to explain to you.

ON A WEEKDAY

He wakes up at around 7 a.m. Reads newspaper while having tea. Puts on a news or music channel on the television and gets ready for work. Drives a sedan to work from XYZ area to ABC area. Reaches office. Opens Outlook, Facebook and Gmail. Uses various applications on his mobile phone throughout the day like Facebook, Twitter, gaana.com, naukri.com, WhatsApp, Skype, etc. Goes to the cafeteria for lunch with his colleagues. Leaves office by 6.30 p.m. via the same route and reaches home. Spends some time with family over evening tea. Reads newspaper or watches news again. Watches daily soaps or entertainment shows or movies. Has dinner. Goes for a small walk after dinner in his apartment complex. Returns home and goes off to sleep by 11 p.m.

ON A WEEKEND

On Saturdays, he generally wakes up a little late, say around 8.30 a.m. Hangs out at home with family over tea, newspapers, breakfast, etc. Takes care of some house-related work, if any, or watches TV. He has lunch, followed by a small afternoon nap. Either goes out with family to a shopping mall or a restaurant or to a nightclub with his friends/colleagues. Sunday is a day of relaxation for him. He stays at home most of the time. Might go out for grocery shopping in the evening, and spends the rest of the evening watching entertainment channels on television or reading a newspaper/magazine/book. Sleeps by 11 p.m., ready for a working week ahead.

Now, when you look back at this person's lifestyle, you can figure out various ways to reach out to his mind space while he lives his life.

On Weekdays

1. Newspapers/magazines
2. News/music channels
3. Outdoor media that he comes across while he drives to-and-fro office
4. Radio channels that he listens to while driving
5. Facebook, Gmail, Google, etc.
6. His office Intranet
7. Various applications on his mobile phone
8. TV screens in his cafeteria
9. A stall set-up/standee/poster in his cafeteria
10. Society activities

ON WEEKENDS

1. Newspapers/magazines
2. News/music/entertainment/movie channels on television
3. Outdoor media
4. Activities/events inside a mall
5. Movies and movie theatres
6. Activities/promotions at restaurants/clubs

These ways that we have listed for our potential customer here, and many others like him, are known as 'Media Vehicles'.

> *Any way or means that helps you reach your potential customer/consumer's mind space is called a Media Vehicle, excluding word-of-mouth publicity.*

So, let us list out various media vehicles that are generally utilized by various marketers as per their categories:

1. ATL (Above the Line)

- Electronic Media (television, radio, etc.)
- Print Media (newspapers, magazines, etc.)
- Outdoor Media (billboards, gantries, TV screens near lifts, etc.)
- Digital Media (Internet-based, social media-based, applications, etc.)

2. BTL (Below the Line)

- Events (concerts, expos, launches, etc.)
- Activations[1] (stalls, human banners, flyer distribution, newspaper inserts, etc.)

---

[1]Activations is where there is an active engagement with the customer. Elaborated on in later chapters.

If you are wondering about ATL and BTL, then the basic difference between these two types of media vehicles is that the probability of a product/service or its representative to be physically in touch with the potential customer/consumer in BTL is very high while that's not at all a possibility in ATL. BTL can be a two-way communication whereas ATL cannot be two-way except in the case of digital media.

Needless to say, this is not a technical definition for ATL and BTL. That you can get from Google. So, I am not getting into the theoretical versions of it. What I am trying here is only to make life easy for you as a marketer.

Chapter five

Reaching Your TG through Various Media Vehicles

This is, practically, what differentiates you from other marketers. This is the reason why you undergo so much training and practice as a marketer.

How do you utilize various media vehicles to reach and influence your TG to buy your product/service?

What do you want to communicate to your TG and how to hold their attention long enough to influence their mind? The most important thing to remember here is that whatever you choose to communicate, it should be same across all the media vehicles used.

Selection of media vehicles for your campaign will depend on two key points:

1. Best vehicle suitable for your communication.

(For example: if you have too many details to communicate, then outdoor media might not be a good media vehicle. Maybe digital media and stall space at expos/cafeterias are a better medium for you. Even Video Ads are a good option in this case—TVC or YouTube.)

2. How much will a media vehicle cost? (TV ads and national print campaigns need very heavy investments whereas digital media or activations are less costly.)

The way you communicate through each media vehicle is the art of marketing. For example:

1. **Television**—This is one of the best mediums if you have a mass product that needs mass appeal. Within masses, it allows you to differentiate your TG reach based on the type of channels you focus—entertainment, news, movies, music, sports, etc. for your specific audience. Television is the most effective medium to create brand space in your consumer's mind along with the fact that videos allow you to explain your offering in the best possible manner due to the audio-visual combination. However, in today's competitive times, you need to ensure that your content grabs your customer's attention within first few seconds,

or he will change the channel. Biggest factor in improving ad viewership is its entertainment value or emotional connect.

2. **Radio**—While I am driving and have my radio switched on, I am constantly changing channels and searching for music. Most of the time, I neither want to listen to the RJ nor the ads. I am sure, that's the case with most of us. So, again, the first five seconds of your ad on the radio need to have some punch to be able to hold your customer/consumer's attention and refrain him from changing the channel. (For example: if your ad starts with a line 'Don't be an idiot to change the channel...' or 'Hi, I am your sofa and I am tired of stinking...' or the voice of a celeb, etc., it has more probability of being heard by the TG.)
3. **Outdoor Media**—In general, the attention span towards a roadside hoarding is not more than 3–5 seconds. It's a little higher for a TV screen above a ticket counter, or in a café, or near a lift. For TV screens, same rules apply as for television communication. However, for hoardings, it is extremely important to focus on an attractive image, bright and easily visible colours, less text, big and easily readable fonts and visible call-to-action. Too much information on a hoarding kills its purpose.

4. **Digital Media**—We are living at the beginning of the Digital Age. Every business is now shifting focus towards digitalization and higher utilization of the digital space. This has also lead to a more informed and smart customer, who unfortunately has a very short attention span. But that's the potential customer you are trying to lure via your marketing campaigns. In such a scenario, digital media is still the most economical medium available currently to reach out to your TG—be it locally, nationally, or for that matter even internationally.
5. **Events**—This medium has the highest possibility of retaining a potential customer's attention span. However, it requires more effort than other mediums do and has lower frequency in a year. An event occurs for an evening, a day, a week or maximum for a month; not more than that. A brand's participation in an event is purely for 'brand awareness' and 'lead generation' purpose. The level of participation in these events would also depend upon whether it is a musical concert, or an expo, or a fair, or a play, or some other local/social event.
6. **Activations**—This is the most personal medium of marketing. Like the *Cinderella* movie photo-op

activations in multiplexes or a credit card company's small kiosks set at the entrance of an ATM or a shopping centre, activations touch a potential customer personally. Most of the activation ideas overlap with the concept of direct marketing. Hence, it is the most influential. The more detailed you are in your activations planning for locations, set-up, manpower, design, interaction dialogue, script, etc., the higher are the chances of someone liking your product and, hence, the brand. If they like it, they will remember and buy it too.

Hope this helps you in achieving a broader understanding of each media vehicle you have in your ammunition kit as a marketer.

We shall look closer and deeper into each of these media vehicles in terms of planning and execution in the next few chapters.

chapter six

Marketing Budget

It might seem like we are jumping topics from one to another without any correlation between them. But that is not the case.

As a marketer, there is no point getting into the utilization of any of the media vehicles unless you are aware of a complete marketing budget for the year. This is where the tricky part comes in for most of the organizations and they usually go wrong due to lack of internal coordination.

Marketing plan in any organization should start with one number in mind, which is:

TOTAL SALES TARGET FOR THE YEAR

The sales target is set by most of the organizations in the form of a percentage, usually ranging between

10 to 30 per cent above the previous year's target. The sales target should not be just a percentage above last year's but should also keep in mind the various other influences on the business like the government policies for the sector, market dynamics and projections for the sector, competition, last year's achieved sales, available sales team, etc. Once again you will notice that most of the organizations do not have detailed research, analysis and discussions before setting up sales goals for the following year, and that's where they either fail to achieve or achieve lower than their potential. You can intervene at this juncture and suggest your colleagues or bosses to take this extra care while setting up a yearly target for your organization.

Nevertheless, once a yearly target is set, it needs to be divided into monthly sales targets based on the usual market demand from experience. For example: a retail company will always have higher sales during the months of August, November and January in India. This is because August and January are EOSS (End of Season Sale) and October is the festive month of Diwali and Dussehra in India. These months of 'highs' can be different from country to country based on its culture and people's shopping habits. For a real estate company Akshaya Tritiya, Gudi Padwa, Dussehra, Diwali, etc., related months are high sales months since it is considered auspicious to purchase land or houses in those days or months. On the other hand, March is a bad month for retail as well as real estate since it's the end of a financial year and people are busy doing tax calculations and filings.

So, you divide yearly sales target into monthly sales targets. Now, as a marketer your work starts with planning a marketing strategy to achieve those numbers every month. This procedure is true for most of the businesses except few unique business models like education, entertainment industry, etc.

There are two ways in which companies deal with this situation:

Fixed Marketing Budget

This is where companies decide upon the yearly marketing budget based on a simple formula:

MARKETING BUDGET = X % OF THE SALES TARGET

(where 'X' can range from 5 to 15 based on the business norms)

In such cases, a fixed marketing budget is given to the marketer, which he needs to spread and spend across the year to achieve the given numbers.

For example: in the real estate industry where the

projects range from a few crores to thousands of crores, the total marketing budget for the whole project is usually 2–8 per cent of the total sales expected from it. This amount is then further divided into a three-year budget since it is not expected that all the flats will be sold in the first year itself. So, for a 100 crore project, the total marketing budget at 5 per cent will be 5 crore. Out of this amount, the first year will consume 2.5 crore, the second year will consume 1.5 crore and the third year will consume 1 crore. By the end of the third year, the project is expected to be sold out.

Unlike the real estate industry process mentioned above, for industries like retail, manufacturing, pharmaceuticals, etc. marketing budget is calculated for that financial year only, not for 2 or 3 years. So, if your annual target is 20 crore, at 10 per cent, your marketing budget will be 2 crore for the year.

Such a calculation process, in my view, is not an intelligent way of allocating yearly marketing budgets and leads to a lot of dissatisfaction and pressure on a marketer. However, some companies prefer it in order to control the final price for the consumer.

Derived Marketing Budget

This is an intelligent way to arrive at a marketing

budget based on logical calculations and market analysis.

Here, based on the monthly sales targets, the TG, the price and the best time of purchase for the customer, you come to a detailed marketing and promotion plan including all the media vehicles required to be able to be confident of achieving the targets. At the end of the day these are purely speculative in nature, but are based on the industry experience and exposure to various marketing and branding techniques of a marketer.

Based on these marketing and promotion plans, media budgets and BTL costs are estimated and added for every month to derive the final marketing budget required for that year to comfortably achieve the sales target at hand.

This figure is then compared with the benchmark figure of 'X per cent of sales target' that the organization is ready to spend comfortably. If the estimated amount is lower than the percentage, the organization is more than happy to go ahead with the derived marketing budget. However, if the derived marketing budget is higher than the comfort figure of the organization, then it should be debated professionally among the top management to come to a pragmatic and acceptable conclusion.

chapter seven

Planning the Annual Marketing Budget

As discussed in the last chapter, we can either have a fixed marketing budget or a derived marketing budget. However, the annual marketing budget must be planned month-by-month and then further day-by-day.

Although there is no formula for this but generally the budget distribution towards various marketing activities is as below:

1. Electronic Media	25 per cent
2. Print Media	20 per cent
3. Outdoor Media	15 per cent
4. Radio Promotions	6 per cent
5. Digital Media	10 per cent
6. BTL	12 per cent

7. Branding and Collaterals 8 per cent
8. Others 4 per cent

This is a yearly distribution and may vary on a month to month basis. But, the final calculation for the year lands close to the above figures for most of the companies.

To create a marketing calendar, you need to first make sure that you have all the events, activities, festivals, special occasions, etc. listed on your calendar. This would mean highlighting all the dates that will influence the shopping behaviour of your TG. Besides all the festivals, these could include summer vacations for kids, long weekends, store anniversaries, expos, fairs, etc.

All these events decide upon the highs and lows of your final sales achievements, as these are important occasions influencing the buying behaviour and spending capacity of your prospective customer. Based on these dates and the other regular weekdays/ weekends falling in that month, you will need to finalize various ways in which you would like to reach out to your TG. In case of a derived marketing budget, all this information is already available to you for each month since you have brainstormed over it in the beginning of the year. And, all you need to figure out then is the smartest and the most cost effective way to execute the plan. We will discuss this in detail for every activity mentioned above, further in the book.

You can prepare your own format of how you would like to have a monthly marketing calendar for yourself. Table I shows a generic monthly calendar in the format that I generally use to plan my marketing activities for the month. Hope this will give you a better visual idea of what we discussed in this as well as the previous chapter.

Your usual marketing calendar will be an Excel document with the first sheet as the summary sheet and the rest of the sheets as a detailed calendar for every month, as shown in the table. The final figures from each month ('sum of all actuals' in Table II below) should directly get reflected in the summary sheet without manual entry.

Table I is a sample of a monthly marketing calendar format. It's a general format that I had prepared for my own personal use, but is eligible for all product/ service marketing with further customization by the users as per their requirements.

Marketing Calendar – June, 2017

Mon	Tues	Wed	Thur	Fri	Sat	Sun
			1: Ads on News Channels	2: Ads on News Channels	3: Ads on Entertainment Channels	4: Ads on Entertainment Channels; Ads in Cinema Screens
5: Ads on News Channels	6: Ads on News Channels	7: Ads on News Channels	8: E-Newsletter Ads on News Channels	9: Hoardings Up; Ads on News Channels	10: Half Page Ad in *Pune Times*; Ads on Entertainment Channels	11: Ads on Entertainment Channels; Ads on Cinema Screens
12: Ads on News Channels	13: Ads on News Channels	14: Ads on News Channels	15: Emailer; Ads on News Channels	16: Ads on News Channels	17: Full Page Ad in *ToI*; Ads on Entertainment Channels	18: Ads on Entertainment Channels; Ads on Cinema Screens
19: Ads on News Channels	20: Ads on News Channels	21: Ads on News Channels	22: *Pune Mirror* skybus; Emailer; Ads on News Channels	23: *Pune Mirror* skybus; Ads on News Channels	24: *Pune Mirror* skybus; Ads on Entertainment Channels	25: Hoarding Ends; *Pune Mirror* skybus; Ads on Entertainment Channels; Ads on Cinema Screens
26 Ads on News Channels	27 Ads on News Channels	28 Ads on News Channels	29 Ads on News Channels	30 Ads on News Channels		

Notes:
9th: Hoarding campaign starts.
25th: Hoarding campaign ends.
Arrows: Period during which hoarding campaign is on.

Table II: How to calculate the respective spends for the above marketing calendar.

Marketing Cost				
Particulars		**Budget**	**Actuals**	**Details**
Electronic Media		**x1 + y1**		
a) E Ad 1	x1			
b) E Ad 2	y1			
Print Media		**x2 + y2 + z2**		
a) P Ad 1	x2			
b) P Ad 2	y2			
c) P Ad 3	z2			
Radio	x3	**x3**		
Outdoor Media	x4	**x4**		
Digital Media	x5	**x5**		
BTL		**x6 + y6 + z6**		
a) Activity 1	x6			
b) Activity 2	y6			
c) Activity 3	z6			
Branding & Collaterals		**x7 + y7 + z7**		
a) Brochures	x7			
b) Leaflets	y7			
c) Flex Printing	z7			
PR	x8	**x8**		
Events (Event Budget)	x9	**x9**		
Agency Retainer	x10	**x10**		
Misc. & Gifts	x11	**x11**		
TOTAL	**Sum of all above**	**Sum of all above**	**Sum of all actuals**	

1. In the first column, you can mention respective ads/activities planned in the category.
2. In column two, you can mention the respective budgeted cost for that ad/activity.
3. Column three is just section–wise total of column two's individual entries.
4. Column four is for filling in actual spends as and when the final bills arrive.
5. Column five is for any specific details about that row's element that you may want to mention for your clarity later.

This covers our top-level topics of marketing.

Let us now get into specific and detailed topics for your better knowledge of execution on the ground.

chapter eight

Planning and Making an AV/TVC

From here, we are moving towards the topics related to execution. So far, we were just planning. Now is the time to get into the relatively less glamorous side of marketing.

When I say AV here, I mean an Audio-Visual presentation. It can be in the form of a TV Commercial or a corporate film or anything else requiring audio and video to communicate your message to the viewer. Planning and creating an AV can be done through multiple ways based on the resources available within your company and with your concerned agencies. However, I am trying to stick to what you would generally do as a marketer.

The most important part of using TV as a medium is that it allows you to tell a story—something that most of the other mediums can't provide. Secondly, it still gives you an ability to reach the remotest pockets of India. These exclusive features allow TVCs to build the values of a brand you are managing.

How to make an AV/TVC

Step 1: Freeze a budget that you would like to keep aside for this AV, along with some additional contingency buffer.

Step 2: Discuss internally as to what is it that you want to convey through this AV and who the viewer is. Also, try to get an idea as to how long would you like this AV to be. If the AV is a TVC it can be of anywhere from 10 to 60 seconds. However, if it is a corporate film, it can be of 3 to 10 minutes. In case, it is some kind of tutorial, it can be even longer based on the content.

Step 3: With this clarity of thought, you should brief your chosen advertising agency or the production house (if they have a copywriter) to come up with a few themes to go ahead on this project.

Example: If you have a social message that you want to pass on to the viewers, it can either be done using a video with voice-over in the background or by way of a conversational act with a complete set-up. The more suitable option of the two depends on the budget that you have finalized for the AV.

Step 4: Based on your brief and the budget constraints, agency will ideate on a few ways in which the message can be put across. If the budget is low then this can be done using images and infographics, and if it's high then using complete shoot and background music plus voice-over.

Step 5: Upon approval on a theme, the agency will provide a story board and share it with you for approval. It's a step-by-step narration of the AV with visual ideas, conversations and voice-over/ background music written in parallel for a wholesome imagination.

Step 6: After approval on the story board, you should sit with the agency to figure out the details of the shoot (if any) or the content of the AV using existing images and infographics.

Example: If the AV involves shoot, the production house will take care of the entire set up and manpower for it. You as a marketer will have to be involved in selection of various actors/models/characters involved and suggesting suitable clothes to the stylist on board to resemble the character sketch of your target group.

In case the AV requires shooting with the employees and top management, you will need to make a schedule for the number of days it will take you to finish the entire shoot and allocate time internally to the staff to avoid delays.

Step 7: Once the shoot is done, the production house will take some time in editing the whole flow and then putting a suitable background score to it. This can either be purchased from an existing collection or can be completely developed by hiring a music director for the job. In the same way, if the AV requires a voice-over (VO), you can ask the production house to share samples of various VO artistes with their cost to decide upon the final VO for your AV.

The copy for the VO will also be given to you by the agency designing the story board. This, of course, will be based on the key messages that you would like to deliver to the audience through this AV.

Step 8: Once the first cut of the AV is ready, the agency will share it with you and you can suggest them final changes, if any.

Step 9: The AV is then delivered to you by the agency in DVD format with 2–3 versions of it in terms of time. So, a 3-minute AV will be accompanied by 2 and 1 minute cut versions as well. Or, cut versions of any other time durations as per your requirement.

Your AV will then be ready to be used as a TVC, or to be played at various conferences or at events where you have sponsored, or at other places providing LED displays/projectors as a medium of communication.

While planning broadcasting spots for your TVC, please remember that time plays an important role. There is a difference in the number of viewers based on what time of the day it is. Hence, prime time is always the costliest due to higher number of viewership during that time. However, you can also be more specific about your ad spot timings depending on your ad's content.

Example: If a Bournvita ad is showing kids playing in it, the time to air it will also be when kids usually go out playing. This will register more in a mother, who would be the TG in this case.

Also, while booking spots for a new ad, you can book spots for a complete ad (45–60 seconds) for the initial 7–10 days. However, later you can shift to frequency builder versions of 20 or 15 secondages.

Points to consider:

1. Before finalizing a production house, please ensure you see their previous work and visit their facility where the final production will happen.

2. Please feel free to give them themes if you have any in your mind, as part of your brainstorming.
3. Please ensure you do not select any actors/models/characters without holding auditions or without a personal meeting, unless the production house has worked with them earlier.
4. Do not hesitate to ask the agency for iterations or corrections during the editing for as many times as you feel to reach the final quality expected.
5. Production houses will ask for a 50 per cent advance payment and rest on delivery of the final approved AV, which is a standard practice. Never agree to pay a higher advance than this.

Go on now, make your first AV/TVC!

chapter nine

Planning and Executing a TV Campaign

Once you have completed preparing a TVC following the steps mentioned in the last chapter, the next step is to put it to use. This is when you would look at the electronic media i.e. TV or cinema screens or LED/ LCD screens used for outdoor media. Let's focus on TV right now, as others are covered in further sections.

Marketing on TV can be of three types:

1. National level
2. State level
3. Local level

National level TV campaign will consider only those TV channels which are to be telecasted to the audience available to them from all over the country. State level TV campaigns focus only on those channels which are regional in nature and focus only on specific states. And, local TV campaigns are done through cable operators or through local city channels.

The reason to pick one of the above completely differs from business to business depending on the product/service involved and the TG it caters to. So, let's look at the way a TV campaign is planned for a business.

PLANNING

Step 1: Based on your TG, you will figure out whether to use national, regional or local TV channels.

For example: If you are an FMCG or electronic goods company with presence all over the country, it's best to use national level TV channels, and also regional TV channels for a deeper reach. Whereas, if you are a real estate company or any product company with distribution base limited to a few regions and not the whole country, then you should opt for regional and local channels. Local channels, on the other hand can be used by local builders, shops, jewellers, schools and other local businesses.

The local channels have their own way of working from location to location, so it won't be possible to discuss them further here. But yes, those are the lowest cost medium within the universe of broadcast media.

Step 2: Once you decide the national or regional way forward, the next thing to decide upon is the genre of TV programmes; you can utilize entertainment channels, news channels, spiritual channels, kids' channels, music channels, sports channels, movie channels or any other.

This is where you will have to go by your own experience of the sector or the industry analysis of various channels utilized by the other players in your category and the budget you have for TV campaigning. Generally, the rates for TV ad spots vary based on the time of the day they are telecasted apart from the type of category chosen. So, entertainment channels usually have the highest ad spot rates during the prime time, followed by movie channels, music and sports channels. Children's, adventure, etc. channels come next. The ad rates for news and spiritual channels are the lowest.

The ad rates for TV campaigns are generally calculated in seconds and secondages. And, ad commercials, as you know, can range anywhere from 5 seconds to 60 seconds or more. Of course, the rates are completely ruled by the 'TRPs'. We all are familiar with this word TRP—Television Rating Point. While some like to debate on the exactness of how TRP is calculated, it is the only organized tool available to measure audience of a TV programme. TRP is calculated with the help of data provided by a device called 'People Meter'. This device is attached to the TV sets of few thousands of viewers' houses purely for monitoring their TV watching behaviour. This data then feeds the TRP tool and gives analytics. In India, this is officially done by INTAM (Indian Television Audience Measurement) agency.

Your choice of a TV channel as a marketer will once again boil down to your TG and channel/ programme's TRP, whatever your budget may be. Few examples have been given below:

Example 1: If your TG is men above thirty years of age, you would generally have a choice between entertainment, news, sports and other generic channels like Discovery, Nat Geo, etc. However, if you have budget constraints, you would want to focus on news channels to get higher mileage within the limited amount possible for you to spend. Within news channels too you need to decide among English, Hindi or a regional language. For an urban TG, you might want to take English channels, for tier I or tier II or rural TG, you might want to pick between Hindi and other regional channels.

Example 2: If your TG is housewives above thirty

years of age, you would generally have a choice between entertainment channels, music channels and spiritual channels. You can also look at Hindi/English movie channels depending on your TG detailing. In all cases, entertainment channels are the best bet to reach women. However, with lower budgets, you can always try music channels or spiritual channels depending on your TG.

Within these channels, you need to know what spots to choose to reach your TG. For men in Example 1 above, it might be evening time from 8 to 9.30 p.m. since they generally watch news during that time. For non-working women in Example 2 above, it might be afternoon hours. For working women, it might be evening slot between 8 and 10 p.m.

I can go on and on with many more examples but what you should aim at is finding what works best for you in terms of cost-effectiveness and final expected results, by doing many trial and error campaigns. You must device specific mechanisms to measure responses to your media campaign to be able to understand what works for you. We will talk about that later in this book.

This is where your sector-specific experience and knowledge comes into picture, and as you grow further in life as a marketer, companies start looking for industry-specific candidates for senior level positions. So, you should be very careful about the sectors you choose as you grow in your career.

Media Rates

Here is how the TV media rates are at present (more or less). These rates are subject to your negotiations with the TV channels and the kind of deals that you crack with them. But the indicative figures below might help you understand how much TV media buying for your campaign can cost you approximately.

English news channels	₹9,000 per 10 seconds
Hindi news channels	₹4,000 per 10 seconds
Business news channels	₹3,000 per 10 seconds
Music TV channels	₹2,000 per 10 seconds
Hindi entertainment TV channels	₹10,000 per 10 seconds
Topic-based English TV channels	₹2,500 per 10 seconds

PLEASE NOTE: The above rates are based on my knowledge of the media. It can be completely different by the time you read this book. The media rates vary from client to client based on the negotiations and relations with the channel. There is no fixed rate that can be given for channels. Card rates are skyrocketing and are only referred to at the time of barter deals. Actual rates are at least 1/4th of the card rates and then it's all about negotiations based on the size of the deal.

EXECUTION

Step 1: Based on your campaign budget, target group and TV channels shortlisting with respect to their reach, TRP and spot rates, you can either come up with a media plan yourself or can brief your ad agency to share a few plans with you.

Step 2: The channel/agency will generally give you a schedule which will be followed to telecast your ad. This schedule is generally not as exact as it's said on paper, but give or take 10 minutes and your ad would appear on the channel as per the schedule.

Step 3: This is when you share your TVC with the channels and they upload the same through their scheduling team. The TVC creation process has been explained in chapter 8 on how to make an AV/TVC.

Step 4: Once the ad campaign starts, you will have to constantly monitor if the ad is telecasted as per the schedule and then monitor impact of the campaign on your sales or achievement of what your target is. This is explained further in the book.

chapter ten

Planning and Executing a Print Media Campaign

Print advertising has been the most conventional advertising medium since long and has still not lost its effectiveness.

PLANNING

Planning a print ad campaign needs you to again have a good knowledge of your TG, and the kind of newspapers/magazines/news categories he/she might be interested in. For print ad campaigns, your usual choices would be:

1. Newspapers – dailies/weeklies
2. Magazines – weeklies/fortnightly/monthlies

3. Trade media (media-specific to the industry/ trade)

Newspapers

Newspapers are widely used for this purpose, especially where it concerns mass advertising. Within newspapers, you will have various choices—English, Hindi and regional dailies.

However, in any language, newspaper as a media vehicle is characterized by its circulation and readers' demography.

For example: In Pune, the highest circulation among all the newspapers is that of *Sakaal*.[1] After *Sakaal* comes *The Times of India* and its circulation is less than half of *Sakaal*'s circulation. *ToI* has *Pune Times* as a supplement and *Pune Mirror* as a tabloid along with the main paper. *Sakaal* has *Sakaal Times* and *Pratibimb* as supplements.

The difference between these two newspapers, however, is in their readers' demography. There is a little overlap in the readers for both. While *ToI* will give you inroads to more cosmopolitan, liberal and modern families, *Sakaal* will help you enter conventional and conservative Maharashtrian families. Both these TGs

[1]http://pune.releasemyad.com/newspapers/education

have enough purchasing power for any kind of product. But, the question is, what is your focus? Whom do you want to reach? And, what is your budget? (*Sakaal* rates for print ads are approximately 3 times that of *ToI* in Pune!)

The above example only takes two publications to showcase the choice of right media for your brand. However, there are many more newspaper choices available to a marketer. You have *Hindustan Times, Loksatta, Lokmat,* etc. in Maharashtra. Similarly, there are other dominant newspapers in various regions in India like the *Deccan Herald* and *The Hindu* in the South, *Rajasthan Patrika* and *Dainik Bhaskar* in central India, and many more.

Your print media plan must be planned in such a manner that with effective utilization of media of regional dominance, you reach out to the maximum of your TG with least amount of marketing money spent from your budget. This is true not only for print media plan but for any marketing plan that you make using any media vehicle.

Newspaper media rates are calculated on square centimetre (sq cm) basis everywhere. The sq cm rate varies within a newspaper based on the page number, page side, main issue, supplement and innovations depending on the publication.

Following are a few jargons, which you would deal with for the rest of your life as a marketer or a business man:

1. **Quarter Page:** 400 sq cm (in a regular-sized newspaper).
2. **Half Page:** 800 sq cm (in a regular-sized newspaper) (to be precise—32.9 cm × 26 cm).
3. **Full Page:** 1,700 sq cm (in a regular-sized newspaper) (to be precise—32.9 cm × 52.5 cm).
4. **RSP:** Right Side Page (usually considered better since analysis shows that readers first look at the right side pages of a newspaper while flipping through it).
5. **LSP:** Left Side Page.
6. **Full Jacket:** Every page has two surfaces—front and back. When both the surfaces of the first as well as the last page of a newspaper are taken by a single advertiser, it is called a full jacket. Even if you imagine it pictorially, it's like a jacket for the rest of the pages of the newspaper.
7. **Half Jacket:** This is quite similar to full jacket, just the page width for both the first and last page is reduced to half. You can imagine it as a sleeveless jacket for the rest of the pages.
8. **Front Jacket:** Only the first page is taken by an advertiser with both its surfaces—front and back

surfaces (page 1 and 2 only).

9. **Skybus:** The top strip just below the name of the newspaper on the front page, almost 5 cm in height and as wide as the page width.
10. **Bottom Strip:** The bottom strip on the front page, placed opposite to the skybus, however, it's a little more in height.
11. **Ad Position:** Page and the position where your ad was placed by the publication. You might have to fight for the best position for your ads as a marketer sometimes.
12. **Ad Quality:** There will be little difference in the ad quality from what you will see on your laptop screen and what will be printed in the newspaper. You must ensure that the quality is best possible and colours, texts, etc. are not altered too much.
13. **Insertion:** The number of times you want your ad to appear is called an insertion. So, if you have given a copy of the ad to the publication and want it to appear on Friday and then Saturday, it will be two insertions. (Please don't confuse it with Paper Inserts.)
14. **Material Deadline:** The deadline for you to submit your ad creative to the publication.
15. **Bleed Space:** This is relevant in case of magazines/ brochures/reports. You need to ensure you know

the bleed space for your creative, for it's a part of your ad that otherwise might get cropped during binding as it won't fit in the scheme of things.

For more details on newspaper advertising and various display ad options, you may visit—http://www.releasemyad.com/newspaper-display-booking/timesofindia/City%20Times/pune.

EXECUTION

Step 1: Based on the ad rates you receive for your choice of newspapers, campaign budget and the number of days of your campaign, decide on your print ads plan. Sometimes, an ad agency might not do the best job in negotiating for rates, so you should intervene and talk to the publications directly to get the best rates for yourself.

Step 2: In your plan, you will have to play with things like ad size and insertion day. Generally, marketers prefer Saturdays and Sundays to be able to reach out to a larger audience. You would generally like to plan an 'Opening Ad' and a 'Closing Ad' for your campaign and try to have few more insertions in between to cover larger readership through various publications. To book your space, you must plan at least 7 days before the insertion date. Get internal approvals and approve the media estimate provided by your agency for the ad.

Step 3: In parallel, you should also brief the agency on the campaign and ask them to share a few campaign ideas and ad creatives for approval.

Step 4: Your ad creative will have to be planned based on whether you are planning a strategic campaign or a tactical one. Strategic campaign is not done with focus on sales. It is primarily focused on branding your company or product, company vision, mission, values, etc. On the other side, a tactical campaign is made with prime focus on sales. It will showcase products/service details, offers, etc. to lure the readers into making a purchase. Ensure there is an evident call-for-action in your ads and the content is put as per your brand guidelines and best readability (font type, size, colour, placement, etc.) of the readers within the time span spent on the ad.

Step 5: Once your ad campaign is set and your ad creatives are approved internally, you can allow the agency to submit your ad to the publications. Please ensure that only an accredited agency is hired by you to do that.

Step 6: You should then monitor the impact of your campaign during the campaign dates and change it if required to ensure maximum ROMI. Details of this are discussed in a further chapter in the book.

If you are a B2C marketer, there is a very high chance that you will be going for a lot of print ads. Please ensure you read everything in your final creative because once it's gone, it's gone. Plus, you will always notice that whatever the resources an agency appoints for your job, you as a marketing manager will always be able to find errors overseen by the client servicing person. Try to do trial-and-error with various print media publication options as well as ad sizes to understand what works better for your product.

chapter eleven

Planning and Executing a Radio Ad Campaign

Radio ad campaigns are one of my favourites after the TVCs, of course. They can be super creative, informative and serve as your best tool for brand recall exercise.

Generally, radio campaigns do not have a direct impact on sales. Customers hardly rush to a store after listening to an ad on the radio. But, they can prove beneficial as a recall agent to your already running campaign. So, it is always suggested to complement your TVC/print/outdoor campaign with a few radio spots.

Radio campaigns also help you choose the cities you are interested in addressing. TV channels have now started looking at local advertising as a medium for ad revenues as well and they are working on programmes that can allow them to have different ad spots for different cities as opposed to a national telecast of ads until now.

Here are the things that you need to know to plan a radio ad campaign:

1. **Copy:** You need to have a written script for the ad that will be produced as a radio spot.
2. **Spot:** This is the time that you buy for a single ad on the radio. It could be anywhere from 10 seconds to 60 seconds. Anything beyond gets boring for the audience.
3. **Slot:** Radios generally have 3–4 slots, namely morning slot (7 a.m. to 12 p.m.), afternoon slot (12 p.m. to 5 p.m.), evening slot (5 p.m. to 10 p.m.) and late night slot (10 p.m. onwards).
4. **RODP:** Run of Daypart. Your ad will run anytime during the day with equal distribution in all the above slots.
5. **Mentions:** As a compliment to your ad campaign, you should try and get RJ mentions for your offer during one of their top shows. It can be of 60 seconds at the most.
6. **Tags:** This is a 5–10 seconds spot that you get as a sponsor of any kind to any of their shows.
7. **Road Block:** You can book a certain time of the day where the radio channel only broadcasts your ads during the breaks. No other ads. No other

mentions! Of course, it's quite expensive too.

8. **MVO:** Male voice-over.
9. **FVO:** Female voice-over.
10. **Secondages:** Total number of seconds that you get as a sum of all the spots broadcasted for your campaign.
11. **Studio Set-Up:** When a radio van comes to your venue and covers the event for a longer period like half a day or a full day or even longer, it is called setting up a studio. This is the most expensive of all the options.

EXECUTION

Step 1: After an internal discussion on the purpose of your campaign (tactical or branding), brief your ad agency to share with you a few scripts for the radio ad. You need to be very clear in your brief as to what is it that you are expecting from the radio campaign. Also, what is the spot length that you are looking at and what will be the call-to-action.

Step 2: You also ask your ad agency to share with you a media estimate for 'x' number of days and whether you want to book particular slots or run an all-day campaign (RODP). Based on your budget for radio, you can make changes in the number of spots or number of days and give a final approval to the ad agency. Needless to say, there are various radio channels and their rates vary based on their listenership. Higher the listenership, higher the rates. Please choose wisely as per your budget and radio channel's reach or listenership. (For more on understanding how audience listenership is measured, please visit http://www.tamindia.com/ram_intro.php)

Step 3: Once you approve the estimate sent to you, your ad agency will issue an RO (Release Order) to the radio channel and share few copies of radio scripts with you to select from.

Step 4: You can have an internal discussion and select a copy with changes from your side. Forward the same to the radio channel. Anyone can forward the copy to the radio channel—you or your agency. However, to avoid wasting a lot of time in a three-way communication, I suggest you coordinate with radio channels yourself. In case you are releasing your ad on two or more radio channels, you can send the script to all of them and ask them to share a 'produced' spot with you.

Step 5: The radio channel would need at least 3–4 hours to get back to you with a production of the script as a radio spot, from their internal studio. This is usually done for free and, hence, most marketers prefer to utilize this service. However, in case you have a script that needs a particular voice (may be your brand ambassador) or a particular way of production, you can always take the help of a production house to do that for you at an additional cost. These production houses have professional voice-over artistes, music directors, singers, etc. on board and they can give you an extremely impressive spot that you would be proud of. It, of course, comes with an additional cost.

Step 6: Once your spot is produced, you can choose from any of the spots sent by all the radio channels and ask the rest to play the same on their stations. There might be chances that the spot will exceed the seconds planned per spot. In that case, you will need to coordinate with the respective radio station for changes in the spot. First, you can try to cut a few words from the script and try to fit it in the time limit planned. If that does not work, you will have to rework on your radio plan to either fit within your budget or get approval on additional budget.

Step 7: Once all that is sorted, you are ready to go on air from the following day, as per the schedule planned. The radio channel should share with you a daily schedule for your spots and generally, if you track your ads, they would appear on air in 10 minutes up or down from the scheduled time.

Step 8: Finally, at the completion of your campaign, the bill will be sent to you for processing. We will learn the organized way to do that in a later chapter. Also, of course, you will learn how we can try to calculate success of the campaign in a later chapter.

Few more important points to remember:

- If your campaign requires your audience to revert to you for some prize, you can give that prize to the radio channel and have them distribute it to the winners. Alternatively, you can ask the radio channel to send the winner to your venue to collect their prizes.
- If your campaign includes live spots on radio, you will have an RJ sent to your venue at a particular time you pick, so that he can record some live interactions. These will be on air within the next 30 minutes giving live coverage to your event.
- If your campaign involves a studio set-up, you will have a radio van parked at your venue and an RJ or an anchor taking constant interactions with the visitors/guests and having it broadcasted throughout the time of the studio set-up.

Hope this provides sufficient information for your first radio campaign. Have fun doing it!

chapter twelve

Planning and Executing a PR Strategy

Public Relations or PR—is one of the most underrated media vehicle or marketing tool among the Indian marketers. And, those who know about its power try to usually overutilize it. Sometimes we don't use a facility; we abuse it. That's what marketers end up doing with PR, at times.

Public relations is a very subjective matter. There is no limit to it. It all depends on how much information you would like to make public. So, basically there are two formats of public relations:

1. Media comes to you by itself.
2. Media is pulled by you through external help.

Before we get into details of the above two types, let's get clarity on what really public relations mean to a marketer. There may be other definitions by PR enthusiasts. But, my definition is:

> *PR is a marketing tool to utilize genuine media to pass on genuine information about a brand/company/industry to the readers, viewers and audiences.*

That's another thing that businessmen/politicians/entrepreneurs have started taking advantage of this form of media to pass on skewed information to their stakeholders. However, if used genuinely, PR can prove to be the strongest of all the media vehicles. In laymen terms, PR is what leads to various news articles we read in newspapers, various coverages we watch on news channels and various news/articles we read online about businesses or personalities or movies, etc.

Fun is when media comes to you, and chases you sometimes. However, not all brands have that pull. So, first of all, you should try to do some genuinely amazing work to be able to attract media attention. That will definitely smell like 'success'...real success. However, if you are not able to attract media by yourself or if you have something new to share that media doesn't know about, you need to take the other route—pull media attention through external help.

The 'external help' mentioned above is none other

than the PR agencies at work. All reputed firms have a PR agency on retainer basis with them. These PR agencies take care of your image in 'public' and monitor, plan, execute, showcase all your communication in public media. These agencies also strategize and suggest you the best ways of sharing information for your organization with public/stakeholders.

A PR agency plays a role in the following:

1. **Listings:** Helping you with your basic tactical campaigns. Listings in dailies and websites for your upcoming events, shows, events, offers, etc.
2. **Articles/Coverage:** Approaching various related media houses/publications, by reaching out to their network of journalists/ correspondents via email, calls or a press conference, to feature you/ your brand in related stories in various related media. If yours is a business story, the agency will target business media like *The Economic Times, Business Today, Businessworld,* etc. If it is a customer story, agency will target general media like *The Times of India, Hindustan Times, The Hindu, India Today,* etc. Sometimes, it's a story already planned by a publishing house focusing on your industry and then you try to get a 'quote' from your senior management to slip into the article. Sometimes, the

article is about your industry's specific side and you are required to showcase what you have in that particular area along with details and perhaps a few pictures. Trust me, the deadlines for such an exercise could be pretty nasty in the middle of an already busy day.

3. **Creating a Story:** This is when you inform the PR agency about the various news you have with you that are yet to be disclosed. The PR comes back to you with a strategy on the kind of stories they can create out of that information which will attract media.
4. **Stakeholder Communication:** As per our Government of India rules, if you have a public listed company, you need to put a public notice in local newspapers before conducting your annual meet of Board of Directors. For instance, if you are planning to construct a multiplex at your premises, you need to put out a public notice in newspapers calling for anyone who is against construction of a multiplex at that property. Sometimes, the policies also define the names of newspapers you need to put the notice into, clearly. There are many more such industry specific activities/requirements/ policies where a PR firm can come to your help and guide you to do your best.

EXECUTION

Step 1: Once you are ready with something new that's worthy of media attention, you inform your PR agency about it. Or, if you do not have anything existing but want PR mileage, you call your PR agency, brainstorm and create something that attracts media attention.

Step 2: Based on your PR agency's feedback and your personal experience, you realize whether this is a listing or an article information.

Step 3: If it's a listing and you have given all relevant information to the agency, they will send you a write-up with images they are going to share with the publications for various listings appearing in dailies, weeklies and websites. And that's how your mention will happen in few of the dailies in the next few days.

Step 4: In case of an article, the PR team sets up a press conference and requests all the relevant media persons to attend it. Alternatively, it could take one step at a time and invite selected journalists and give them story pegs via an interview the CEO/MD or company's spokesperson. Information that has not yet been disclosed to the rest of the media is shared during both kinds of events. A copy of the PR brief

(Press Release) is also handed over to the journalists as reference material.

Step 5: After the one-on-one session or the press conference, the PR team keeps a track of the journalists and if they are featuring the story with their publication and when. In most of the cases, journalists cannot be forced to put a story or a review or an article as part of their write-up. It's always based on their interest in the story along with the editor's call of whether the story is worthy of space in their newspaper.

Step 6: You can invite the journalists for wine and dine, also share some gifts, but in PR it can never be confirmed whether your story will still appear in the newspaper or not. Needless to say, your PR agency and its relations with various journalists is the key here to push your stories and time them well.

Step 7: Finally, when your story appears in the news, don't be surprised if it doesn't turn out the way you expected or wanted the message to be delivered. What, for you, is the most crucial information, might not be 'breaking news' material for the media. And, they might feature a small piece of information mentioned casually during the one-on-one meeting as the main news instead of focusing on the communication you are trying to push consciously. They do all this only to ensure they are the first ones to break the news. So, you must be extremely careful and cautious while giving media bytes and answering their questions.

Example: A close friend of mine had a one-on-one meeting with one of his city's most important newspaper's business journalist. The interview was to reveal upcoming plans of the company and during the discussion, my friend casually revealed to the journalist that they are in talks with a foreign company for a collaboration and entry to India but they do not want this information to go public till things are confirmed. What followed next week was a blunder. The reporter took this as inside information and instead of focusing on the information that was meant to be published, he wrote an article with a headline about that foreign company planning to enter India. It spoiled everything for my friend and eventually the foreign company backed out. The deal that was so ripe and ready to be signed, just got buried somewhere and did not come through even after multiple follow-ups. So, learn to be very careful about the information that you want to go out to media and that which should not.

Step 8: Once your story is out in a daily, there is a chance that few other dailies would show interest in covering the story as well. This is how your PR campaigns start and grow organically or inorganically with your PR agency's push. But either way, it's a success if you are featured in the top 3–4 dailies followed by a few more local features. You are home! Plus, if you are in a B2C kind of business where the news could impact customers directly and excite them too, you might get a call from radio channels for an on-air interview. Also, you might also get featured by news channels if your story is interesting to them. These events may occur though not necessarily in that order.

I still remember when I was approached by *DNA*, Mumbai to feature my first start-up venture (Cornucopia Weekend Planners) in the newspaper. It was unexpected and it was an amazing surprise for me. The journalist had found our monthly events 'A Night in a Den', 'Musical Trek', 'Kick Boxing on the Beach', 'Scuba Diving in Mumbai', and more quite interesting at that time and she was following us on Facebook. Once she was sure, she called us. That was the first time ever I was called for any media coverage in my life. I cannot share the joy of accomplishment and pride I felt then.

I gave the interview; they also took a picture of our team and featured it in the newspaper on a weekday. It was unbelievable that, even before I knew that the article was out, I received a call from an RJ Sangeeta from Radio Mirchi telling me that she saw the coverage in *DNA* and she would like to take my interview for their channel. Well, that morning I gave my first ever radio interview sitting at home talking to the RJ on my phone while many Mumbai residents were reading an article about my first venture. The radio channel was obviously recording it and broadcasted it on their channel many times after that. Also, on that day we received more than a hundred calls for membership registration and many more for further information on what we do.

DNA saturday FEATURES

Home of Football

parent TRAP

Roster for fun weekends

An online planner helps you stay clued in about the range of activities and events taking place in the city during weekends

A tale of three cousins

Die-hard supporters and fans of the Arsenal Football Club have come together at the Arsenal Mumbai Fan Club to add more cheers for their team

Gunning for ARSENAL

ART FOR YOUR HOME

Affordable artwork is on display at an exhibition cum sale

That's the power of PR! Of course, I had the opportunity to be featured on *Bloomberg UTV* and *ET*

Now as well. And all this was completely genuine PR without any 'external help' and without a single penny spent.

Make sure you utilize PR. And make sure you utilize it wisely for your business and you will see various benefits. Few of those benefits are as mentioned below:

1. Makes your brand more genuine in the eyes of the customers.
2. Makes your brand more trustworthy in the eyes of the consumers.
3. Helps your sales, if drafted well.
4. Helps your footfall, if detailed well.
5. Helps you get better employees since they see you often in media and aspire to be a part of your organization.

All the best for your rendezvous with PR. I am sure you will enjoy the ride and hopefully, remember me while at it.

chapter thirteen

Planning and Executing an Outdoor Campaign

I was a small-town boy for a long time. Maybe I still am one, deep inside. My family and I, however, used to visit cities like Indore and Gwalior during vacations. When in the city, like all kids, I had this habit of looking outside the car window and observing everything possible. I would always see those big boards across the city with phone numbers written on them in big bold letters, and wonder what these numbers are for.

I would also ask my mother, but she was no marketer and had no clue about it. So, she would say—'*Pata nahi, beta* (I don't know, son).' Little did I know that years later these boards will become such an important part of my career! Well, of course, you know by now that I am talking about the various billboards or hoardings we see across any city. They are part of a whole industry known as 'Outdoor Media Industry'.

Outdoor media industry is still not a very organized one in India. However, it is doing well and is extremely important for all the marketers. My definition for outdoor media is as follows:

> *Any media vehicle that you see once you step out of your home, helping a product or service to reach out to you can be called Outdoor Media or Out of Home (OOH) Media.*

Various types of outdoor media can be broadly categorized as below:

1. Hoardings/Billboards
2. Gantry
3. Bus Shelters
4. Digital Screens (LCD/LED)
5. Pole Signages
6. Horticulture/Management of Public Areas
7. Mobile Vans
8. Vehicle Wraps (Car/Bus/Train/Airplane/Auto/Metro)
9. Bus Branding
10. Transit Media
11. OOH + Mobile Ads
12. Innovation in OOH

However, before we dig deeper into these various types of outdoor media, it's important you understand the following terminologies used for it:

1. **Morning Traffic:** The media is visible to people when they are heading towards work in the morning.
2. **Evening Traffic:** The media is visible to people when they are heading back from work in the evening.
3. **Line of Sight:** The angle at which the outdoor media is visible while a person is driving a bike or a four-wheeler.
4. **FTF:** Facing Traffic From.
5. **FTT:** Facing Traffic To.
6. **Printing:** The cost of printing the flex to be pasted on the outdoor media. This is generally charged at ₹8 per sq ft (it may vary from place to place and vendor to vendor).
7. **Mounting:** The cost of manpower for putting the flex up on the media. This is generally charged at ₹4 to ₹5 per sq ft.
8. **Lit:** Media that has arrangement for light, so that it is visible during the night as well. Costs more.
9. **Non-Lit:** Media that has no lights and hence has low visibility during the night. Costs less.

10. **Front-Lit:** Media on which light is thrown from the front of to the flex.
11. **Back-Lit:** Media on which light is thrown from behind the flex by pasting it on top of a box type structure with lights inside.
12. **Solace Site:** Media which has no other kind of media site next to it leading to a perfect sight without any distraction. Costs more.
13. **Cluttered Site:** Media which is surrounded by many other media assets making it very confusing for a passer-by to register any of the brands present on it. Costs less.
14. **Long Visibility:** Media site that is visible from a long distance and for a long time to the traffic coming towards it. Costs for such sites are higher.
15. **Short Visibility:** Media site that is not visible from a long distance due to blockage by a tree or building or a turn or sometimes by another outdoor media site. Costs for such sites are lower and can be easily negotiated further down.
16. **Normal Flex:** Material that is usually used to print outdoor media creative and mount it on the media site.
17. **Reflective Flex:** This is a better quality, far shinier version of flex that becomes bright and visible when your vehicle lights fall on it. Of course, it's

more expensive too. Almost double the price of normal flex.

18. **Self Adhesive Vinyl (SAV):** Generally used on the outdoor media sites on highways. This is because, the sites on highway have a metal sheet (usually aluminum) in the background and the SAV can be pasted on it. If a flex is mounted on top of a basic outdoor media frame on the highway that has no metal sheet, the wind will tear it apart within a day or two.
19. **Black-back Flex/Vinyl:** This material has a dark black rear side. This helps when you want to mount it at a place with lots of sunlight or electric light in the background. Ensures that the creative is visible clearly without any interference from the light.
20. **Reflective Vinyl:** It is also Self Adhesive Vinyl but has the capacity to shine when light falls onto its surface. Of course, it is more expensive than normal SAV.
21. **Bond:** The adhesive generally used to paste various types of flex on different surfaces. It is super strong and sticks within 3–5 seconds.

DETAILS OF VARIOUS TYPES OF OUTDOOR MEDIA

Bilboards/Hoardings

The media type used in outdoor media by most of the marketers are hoardings. Hoardings can be of various sizes and shapes. But, once you are planning an outdoor campaign, even before finalizing various sites, you can ask your ad agency to work on creatives and have them ready in following aspect ratios:

1. 1:1 (This ratio creative can be easily adapted for hoardings with sizes like 20ft x 20ft, 30ft x 30ft, etc.)
2. 2:1 (This ratio creative will help you for hoardings with sizes like 20ft x 10ft, 40ft x 20ft, etc.)
3. 3:2 (This will help you with sizes like 30ft x 20ft, 60ft x 40ft, etc.)

Of course, hoardings are of other sizes also, but these are the most general sizes used everywhere for erecting a hoarding within a city. On the other hand, if you are looking at hoardings on the highway, the sizes will be far bigger and different. I have seen hoardings that are as big as 200ft x 40ft on highways.

An example of a Solace Hoarding. This one has a long visibility and has no clutter around it.

An example of a clutter of hoardings with all having short visibility with good line of sight. The one on top of the building has bad line of sight.

Also, please remember that the bigger the hoarding, the heavier its print file will be and the longer it will take for the printer to print it on a flex/SAV too. So, if you are planning a hoarding campaign, please give yourself at least two days for the process of printing and mounting. It's not something that you should expect to go live overnight. Not that it's impossible, but generally try to keep some buffer time with you. (Heavy print files will also take a long time for your agency to upload and send you via wetransfer.com or sendspace.com, and the same or more time for your vendor to download it from the direct download link.)

There are strict rules for the construction of hoardings in or outside city by the government and its recommended that once you select hoardings for your campaign, you ask the outdoor media agency to show you the licence or certificate they have for those sites.

Gantry

A gantry is what you would generally see across the road, almost like an arch. These are usually built by the municipal corporations to place direction sign boards for public convenience. However, signage only covers that half of a gantry which is on the side of a divider that is facing the traffic. The other half is of no use to the municipal corporations as the rest half of the traffic has its back towards the gantry.

That's why municipal corporations put tenders out for these outdoor media agencies to take up these spaces and utilize them for advertisements. These tenders are usually for a period ranging from 3 to 5 years. And during this period the outdoor media company needs to pay rent to the municipal corporation irrespective of whether it is able to sell ad space for these sites or not.

An example of a Gantry with ad space available on the opposite side of the approaching traffic.

So, as a marketer, you would like to complement your outdoor media plan with few gantries to spice it up or as an option against an expensive hoarding in that area or even as a direction board for your property/ store/mall. Creatives for gantries are a bit tricky, so please remember the following things while briefing your agency:

1. The sizes for gantries are like 60ft x 8ft, 80ft x 8ft, etc. They are less in height and more in length.
2. Attention span of a passer-by is very short for gantries since they are not tall and are usually on the other side of the divider on the road.
3. Your creative should have less text, but 1–2 images, logo and call-to-action.
4. Also, the text size for any of the outdoor media should be big enough to ensure easy readability in a quick glance.
5. In case, you are planning to use it as a direction board, please keep the arrow on the left side of your creative. It will be closer to the traffic that is going to look at your creative.

Bus Shelters

Bus Shelters are another popular medium used by marketers for advertising/branding. There are various sizes for bus shelters but primarily there will be three components for your advertisement space on a bus shelter:

1. Front top panel (usually the biggest in size)

2. Side top panels (on both sides on top)
3. Background panel (at the rear wall of the bus shelter)

An example of a Bus Shelter with visible back and front top panels.

Please be very clear of what you want to communicate on each of these panels and give a brief to your agency accordingly.

Digital Screens (LCD/LED)

These are those LED/LCD screens that you see while standing in a queue at the local railway station counters or next to lifts or lobbies or at coffee shops and also in fast food joints. Most of the times they are either playing ads or some kind of engagement fillers like 'Did you know?', general FAQs, and more.

These screens generally have a USB inserted in them or are connected via an internet network, controlling them from a central admin panel. Either way, they have the content running on a loop of 8 to 12 minutes usually. The loop length is derived based on the logic that, with such length of the loop, it is believed that the number of eyeballs on each ad is the maximum and, hence, maximum number of passer-bys will see maximum number of ads.

This media has not been very successful in India since it is not easy to calculate the ROMI for these media assets and also there is no way to confirm how many people saw your ad or noticed it. Plus, the logic to costing is also unclear. So, as a marketer, you will really have to be very smart and squeeze the deal at the lowest cost possible.

An example of a Digital Screen installed at a traffic signal.

Although, keep in mind, running your ads on digital screens will always be an 'add-on' to an ongoing campaign and not part of your must-do list.

Pole Signages

In most cities, there are very few outdoor media companies that deal in pole signages. These are those flagpoles that you either see on the dividers at the centre of the road or tied to electricity poles. Generally, a creative on flagpole signage is not very big in size. The biggest that I have seen was 5ft x 4ft. These could be flex/vinyl and back-lit as well.

An example of a Pole Signage.

These are good to use if you are trying to cover your catchment area or if you do not have any other outdoor media source available in a particular area to reach out to your TG. Pole signages serve the best when you would like to own your catchment area and either use branding opportunity on these poles or direction signs for your property.

Horticulture/Management of Public Areas

This is where your public and private sector partnership can be seen as an example. You can approach local municipal authorities asking for permission to manage certain public properties in the city. For example: public toilets, dividers, signals/squares, etc.

You take up full responsibility of those public spaces that you are interested in and make sure they are fully maintained and operational for use by common people. In return, you are allowed to use all the ad space possible on it for your marketing/branding purpose. If it requires landscaping and gardening, that will also be your responsibility as an organization.

Anytime the government bodies think that you are not doing a good job, they can withdraw your rights to take care of the space and to use it for your marketing/branding. Needless to say that dealing with bureaucrats can be more cumbersome than you can imagine while reading this book. So, as a marketer it will definitely help you if you get your hands dirty as soon as possible and learn to deal with various rules and regulations in this regard.

Mobile Vans

While most of the outdoor media is fixed and immobile, mobile vans are the only option you have which is movable as per your daily plan. Mobile vans come in handy when you need to reach out to multiple areas with less spends or areas where hoardings are not allowed.

Laws have become very strict for mobile vans in India lately and you are not allowed to park them wherever you wish to. Nevertheless, staying within the law you can use mobile vans to cover various areas. You should chart out a daily plan for your mobile van campaign with the vendor and ensure that you do enough surprise checks to make sure things are working as planned.

One of the examples of a Mobile Van promotion, placed strategically along a busy road to get maximum eyeballs.

Vehicle Wraps (Car/Bus/Train/Airplane/Autos/Metro)

The latest popular favourite in the outdoor media world are vehicle wraps. A vehicle wrap is not just a part of a vehicle or a panel/sticker acting as ad space on its body. It is the whole of it.

An example of a Vehicle Wrap executed for this brand in Dubai. Courtesy: Encyclomedia Global

The complete vehicle, be it car or bus or a train or even an airplane can now be completely wrapped as if it is advertising your product. This is obviously a good marketing gimmick and it also has a superb reach. These are generally expensive options as well and should be done only if it can be used for a longer period. For examples of vehicle wraps on the Delhi Metro, check out this website: http://delhimetroadvertising.com/

An example of a Bus Wrap executed for this brand in Dubai.
Courtesy: Encyclomedia Global

An example of a Train Wrap executed for this brand in India.
Courtesy: Encyclomedia Global

Also, recently Government of India decided to allow vehicle wraps on Indian Railways as well.[1]

---

[1]http://timesofindia.indiatimes.com/india/pepsi-rajdhani-coke-shatabdi-on-track-railways-readies-plans-to-brand-trains-stations/articleshow/56410832.cms

Bus/Train/Vehicle Branding

These are usually brand panels placed on the walls of a bus or a train. On a bus, these are on the sides as well as on the rear. These can be particularly useful since the local buses and trains travel all over the city and transport a huge city population. You can choose buses based on their route.

Local trains have ad space option inside each compartment as well. Also, a lot of government buses have started having an LCD screen behind the driver's seat used for displaying ads to the commuters. Same is also the case with auto rickshaws and a few taxis nowadays, especially in Pune. (Visit www.myriky.com to see it for yourself.)

An example of Vehicle Branding executed for this brand in Argentina.
Courtesy: Encyclomedia Global

Transit Media

Transit Media usually involves various branding/ marketing opportunities at bus stops, railway stations and airports. Lately, the management and construction companies have started including ad spaces as part of the project plan to give it due credit and avoid wear and tear later. This way most of the media assets at most airports are very well-maintained and do not seem like a force fit.

Airport branding is usually way more expensive than the general outdoor media.

An example of a Bus Wrap executed for this brand.

OOH + Mobile Ads

With the advent of technology, outdoor media or Out of Home Media (OOH), as we call it, has also combined itself to the digital world and, hence, has come up with new solutions.

The billboard recognizes all the mobile phones in its vicinity if their Bluetooth or Wi-Fi is switched on and pushes the same ad as on the billboard or an extension of it to reach out to its TG. This OOH Mobile Network is a customized geo-fencing solution, grounded in OOH assets and is local verification enabled. Please visit www.outfrontmedia.com and look into their 'Mobile Network' section, there is a well-made video also, for your better understanding.

Innovation in OOH

Outdoor media is one field where there is a lot of scope for innovation but needs a lot of hard work and smart thinking as well.

An example of an innovation on a hoarding.
Brand has placed lights on their logo and '100% OFF' offer.
This makes the hoarding stand out!

If you google 'innovative outdoor media' and look at images, you will know what I am talking about. There are multiple ways to innovate concepts in outdoor media and you should try it once too.

Walking billboards is one of the latest examples. It is also known as human billboard. The age-old method of innovation in outdoor media is use of 'cut-outs' which go out of the basic frame of the billboard and make it look like a 3D image. I am sure once you google those images you will be awestruck for a while looking at the kind of ideas that have been executed globally in the outdoor media business.

However, the more innovative the idea, more will it cost you and you will also need to find an agency that will help you execute the idea professionally. Innovation in outdoor media not only increases the number of eyeballs on your outdoor ad, but also makes you the talk of the town. And, definitely gets you a lot of PR mileage and awards if you do something unique.

So, marketers should keep some budget aside every year for investing in 1–2 outdoor media sites for an innovative campaign and create an identity for their brand's style of advertising. Please remember, everyone appreciates innovation.

An example of innovation in OOH executed for this brand in Chile.
Courtesy: Encyclomedia Global

An example of innovation in OOH executed for this brand in Nigeria.
Courtesy: Encyclomedia Global

An example of innovation in OOH executed for this brand in Dubai.
Courtesy: Encyclomedia Global

An example of innovation in OOH executed for this brand in Saudi Arabia.
Courtesy: Encyclomedia Global

An example of innovation in OOH executed for this brand in Peru.
Courtesy: Encyclomedia Global

An example of innovation in OOH executed for this brand in Dubai.
Courtesy: Encyclomedia Global

EXECUTION

Step 1: Once you know that you are looking at an outdoor media campaign or outdoor media presence for long term, first thing you internally discuss is the areas where you would like to be present which helps you reach your TG the most. In case of a national level campaign, please take help of your local sales/ marketing teams to list down important areas to be covered via outdoor media for each city. Also, at the same time, please brief your ad agency to work on creative options and have them ready in various basic ratios as discussed earlier in this chapter.

If it's a national level campaign, you can look at agencies like Global Media, Laqshya Media, Bright Media, Selvel, etc. which have their own assets in most of the cities in India. Or you can approach aggregator agencies like Postorscope, www.myhoardings.com or www.oapindia.com and have them coordinate with various outdoor media companies to give you best locations irrespective of the asset owner. On the other hand, if you know all the outdoor media agencies covering various cities you want to focus on in your campaign and you want to coordinate with them personally, please go ahead. The only issue you will face will be too much coordination and too much headache. For a local (only one city) campaign, it's better to approach local outdoor agencies personally and coordinate further with them.

Step 2: Approach few of the above mentioned agencies or any other agencies and give them a brief in terms of your requirements—number of days, cities, areas, etc. Ask them to send you a media plan as soon as they can. They generally take 1–2 days to send you the plan based on the number of cities involved.

Step 3: Once you receive the plan, you will generally have a presentation with images of various media assets, their sizes, their area, their name and their traffic details. Plus, whether they are lit or non-lit. Along with that you will also receive an Excel sheet listing each of the assets covered in the presentation giving details of their availability and cost. Usually, both are in the same sequence for your clear understanding. You can take the best three plans and discuss them in detail with your internal marketing team, and also share respective city plans with your local teams to get their ideas.

NOTE: Please understand that it's very important as a marketer that you get a buy-in from your local sales teams while doing a local campaign. Otherwise, they will keep blaming your wrong choice of media in case of low sales.

Step 4: Once you have decided on various sites in various locations, you should ideally go on a recce (visit) along with the media agency's sales representative to personally see all the media assets or have your local colleagues do that and report to you whether those are good choices or not. Please remember, it's the job of the media agencies to sell their every asset. So, they always take pictures of their assets from the best angle possible. But the truth comes out only when you actually go and see the site yourself. You should analyse the various points we discussed in the beginning of this chapter before finalizing each site.

Step 5: After the recce, you can give your list of final media sites to the agency and ask them to give you a final quote on the same. Then, spend some time negotiating to bring the cost down to the lowest you can. Also, try to negotiate the starting date for your creative to be up on the hoarding.

Step 6: While negotiations are on, please share the presentation of the final media sites with your ad agency and ask them to adapt the basic creatives made for outdoor media campaign into the various sizes mentioned in the presentation.

Step 7: Share the print files of approved creatives for various hoardings with the outdoor agency in case of a national campaign or with your local printer in case of a local campaign. Execution is easier if you have a central outdoor agency for a national campaign. Just imagine the kind of coordination you will get into if you try to coordinate with various agencies in every city to have your campaign up on the same date in all the cities! It will be overwhelming, I can assure you.

Step 8: Once the campaign is up, your outdoor agency will share with you images of all the media assets with your creative up. Once again, it is suggested that you have a personal supervision of all the assets to see if your flex has been mounted properly and stretched well to leave no creases. Also, visit lit sites one night to see if the lights are working properly and if your creative is visible.

Step 9: Try and analyse your campaign's ROMI, if possible. We will learn more about it in a further chapter.

It takes time to understand how OOH works due to many parameters in play. However, the faster you understand it, better it will be for your marketing career. Also, it's very time consuming.

chapter fourteen

Planning and Making Marketing Collaterals

As a marketer, along with doing the bigger things like managing marketing budgets and designing various campaigns, you will also be doing a lot of small day-to-day things. This chapter tries to list them for you, give you a brief introduction to it, and explains how to go about executing the same.

1. Flyers/Pamphlets

One of the most used marketing collaterals is a flyer or a pamphlet. You can plan these in A5, A4, A3 or as a bi-fold of A3 (4 surfaces) sizes but the most common ones are in A4 size. Again, the quality of flyers also depends on the thickness of paper used. This could range from 90 GSM (minimum) to 170 GSM. It's best to use 110 or 130 GSM art paper with a four-colour printer.

Cost of printing flyers depends on the number of flyers. Higher the quantity, lower the cost. Provided that the design for all the flyers is same. For different designs, your printing vendor will have to create different plates and those will cost you extra, plus the cost of printing will go up since the whole quantity of order will be divided into the number of different designs. Since flyers are printed in a huge quantity, offset printers are the best choice.

Depending on the quantity, the flyers' printing and drying process can take about 1–2 days. So, plan your creatives accordingly. Also, in case you are planning to distribute flyers with newspapers, you must give the flyers to your distribution vendor before midnight, so that they can be distributed along with the newspaper next day. You can also decide areas of distribution and the kind of newspaper, based on readership and your TG with the distribution vendor.

During my flyer campaigns, I used to divide the distribution over 3 days. Thursdays would be for areas in 10 km radius, Fridays would be for areas in 5 km radius and Saturdays for areas in the catchment. You can also try the same method. This way people who are farther from your store/venue get more time to plan a visit to your store.

2. Posters/Certificates

Posters come handy when you are looking at offline affiliate marketing and pasting posters of your event/ offers at various other outlets or schools or corporates, etc. or even selling tickets through those places. Generally, posters can be A4 or A3 in size, 170 GSM or more in thickness on an art paper.

Same is the case with certificates given to employees during annual functions or sports events, etc. Although, usually certificates are only of A4 size. Both are usually printed in smaller quantities and can also be different from each other in design elements. In such cases, digital printing is the best choice. Digital prints also have a shine which offset printing does not have.

3. E-Newsletters

E-newsletters are your weekly, fortnightly or monthly dose of marketing communication with people who are already in your database or have subscribed to your newsletter. There is an 'e' here since these are not printed and only sent in the form of a mailer to the list of recipients that you develop as you grow in email marketing opt-ins. Opt-ins are acquired through various online forms available on your website or emails or any type of landing pages to be filled by users sharing their email IDs for you to send them mailers.

An e-newsletter must have a name and its own logo unit for starters. As part of the body, you can have your latest news, offers, happenings, awards and media coverages in a newsletter. There can be few constant parts in every newsletter like weekly tip, contact details, etc.

Your e-newsletters serve purposes of staying in touch with your existing customers and other stakeholders, and serve as your communication tool to keep all the internal as well as external stakeholders on the same page.

Please make sure you have an attractive subject line for each and every e-newsletter, which ensures that the recipients at least open your mail. And, do have an 'Unsubscribe' option at the bottom of your newsletter. This gives freedom to the recipients to decide whether to continue receiving emails from you or not. This is also the official guideline most of the email servers use by default. And, keep a good mix of text and images in your newsletter to keep it interesting. Also, please make sure all the hyperlinks on your newsletter work and take the recipients to linked pages on your own website and you have relevant content there.

4. Monthly/Quarterly Newsletters

These are hard copy newsletters, which can be created monthly or quarterly and distributed to important stakeholders and potential clients/retailers.

Though these are of limited print runs, creating these newsletters can be one of the most time consuming and detailed tasks for you. Consider it this way that you are the editor-in-chief for the newsletter and the whole and sole person responsible for all the content in it.

Your newsletter can have various sections like cover story, client interviews, customer testimonials, product-based articles, event coverages, tips, upcoming events, industry news, awards and media coverages, and also product information/listings.

Believe me, compiling the data for a newsletter is easier than reading the copy again and again to ensure there are no mistakes nor any wrong or excess information. It's also easy to start producing these newsletters but more difficult to continue producing them every month or quarter without any delays.

5. Standees

There are various types of standees that you will need to make during your marketing journey. However, the most common ones will be of the size 3ft (w) x 6ft (h). These can be of two types:

- Roll-Up Standees: The ones which are made of aluminum, light to carry, and need to be rolled up and fitted using a vertical support stick on the rear side. These are generally useful when you need a quick branding presence at an event/activation and do not have time to produce something new. Or, if you have an opportunity for brand presence in an out-of-city event and you have to carry standees with you in a taxi or a flight.
- MS Frame Standees (Mild Steel): These are made of iron frames welded together with a base to make it self-standing. These are heavier than the roll-up ones but sturdier and are handier when you have branding opportunities in outdoor areas. These cannot be dismantled like roll-up standees once work is done. MS frame standees can, however, be of other bigger sizes also and can be used as backdrops for presentation ceremonies or as camouflage for an under-construction area at your store/mall/venue/project site and more.

Both the types of standees can have their flex replaced and can be used multiple times. So, as a marketer, it is advised that you keep a few roll-up standees ready with you for any urgent branding needs and have a few MS frame standees as inventory to be used for various occasions at your store/venue.

6. Booklets/Books

As a communications manager, it might be desired from you that you manage the annual report or some other kinds of books like an 'Advertising Guide Book' covering all the campaigns done in the past or media coverage acquired by your brand in the past.

Apart from working on the content for these books along with your advertising agency, you will need to also plan whether these will be centre pinned or will have a spiral binding or book binding. You will also need to keep some bleed space in your creatives so that your content does not get lost while binding.

Annual reports are an extremely serious business and I am not going to get into the details of the same here. Offer booklets will be much smaller in size with thicker paper and may need perforations to help tear apart every offer coupon. Perforations increase the total cost of the booklets too.

7. Other Marketing Merchandise

There are various other marketing merchandise that you will need to work on and it's going to be impossible to cover all of those in this book. But, just to give you an idea, you might do some branded corporate gifting, uniforms, caps, t-shirts, table tops, banners, price tags, stationery, and more, as a marketer. There are vendors who specialize in all of these separately and you will have to work with the commercials team of your finance department to find reliable vendors.

Hope you have lots of fun doing these tasks. There will be separate vendors for each of these tasks and you will need to manage multiple vendors and relations with them to get your work done properly and in time.

chapter fifteen

Planning and Executing an Event

As a marketer, you would be required to plan, coordinate and execute many events in your career. These events could be product launches, store launches, brand launches, concerts, dealer meets, conferences, and much more.

There is a high probability that you might not have any event management experience once you start your marketing career or your own business. There will be many people or agencies who might dupe you with various event industry jargons and higher rates for various elements in the cost sheet. This is where your experience and negotiation skills will come into play.

Let's try to capture few of the elements of event management that you will come across.

ELEMENTS FOR EVENT MANAGEMENT

Set-Up

Stage: Stage can be of any size but it will usually have to be a multiple of 8ft x 4ft. That is because, as of now, the base used to prepare stage is made with tables/frames of size 8ft x 4ft. However, you can always find different ways with various vendors for sure. Another aspect of a stage is its height. Usually it is between 1–2 feet for most of the corporate events but around 3–4 feet or more for conferences and concerts. Stage will most often have a backdrop and projector screen as well. These are detailed in below points. The usual cost for a stage is around ₹30 per sq ft per day including carpet.

Carpet: You would generally have a carpet on the stage and around your stage area in an event. Generally, a grey-coloured carpet is used for corporate events. You can always choose some other colour as per your plan or liking. There is also the option of the famous 'red carpet'. For instance, during Indian classical concerts, you would be required to have a white sheet covering the stage with some mattresses and pillows and bolsters in place to help musicians sit comfortably. All in white!

Podium: You would need a podium with a mic for your events if it is a formal or semi-formal set-up. The podium also works as a branding opportunity for you to place your event creative on its front to be featured in all the pictures taken. Most of the modern podiums have a slider to put a poster in it. It is usually A3 in size. Use it wisely with creatives that can be seen from far.

Backdrop: Your backdrop can be of the whole length as your stage or smaller. It could either be made with an iron frame/multiple iron frames or a temporary frame made of flat wooden sticks (called 'batempatti' in India). The creative for backdrop will be printed on a flex and mounted on either of these frames. Please ensure there is no crease on the flex and the frames are stable, and can take a few shakes (if it happens due to a breeze/wind).

Projector: The backdrop could have projector screens placed on either or one side of it. Usually these are of 8ft x 6ft size in order to get best output from the basic projectors used. If you intend to have bigger projection, you need to budget for special projectors with HD quality content played on them. Projectors can be in front or rear based on the space available to you in front or behind the stage. Wherever you place the projectors, please ensure there is a border created between the projector and either side of the screen so that no one can walk in between them and make your event look funny or unorganized. In banquet halls, these can be roof-mounted and hence you won't have to worry about bordering (cordoning off) the area.

Screen: As mentioned above, screens are usually of size 8ft x 6ft. This is the area where projector's light will fall to show whatever is projected to the audience. However, this area is part of a bigger frame like 12ft x 10ft or something similar. This frame will ensure that screen is at least 3–4ft above the ground for better visibility from across the length of the event venue and will also provide branding opportunity for all the brands involved in the event. Hence, usually, screen frames have a flex with all sponsor logos on it with white screen at the top centre. This satisfies your sponsors too. Other types of screens are LCD/LED screens with a digital feed in them used as a backdrop. Those are more expensive though.

LED Par: These are the low intensity round-shaped colourful throw lights used to create a colourful ambience at an event venue. These will usually be used to throw lights on the walls or backdrops to make them look more beautiful. These keep changing their colour as well, if you set them like that. Usually these will cost you approx. ₹200–250 per light per day. You can always negotiate for better rates.

Parcans: These are higher intensity round-shaped colourful throw lights generally used to throw light on the stage area. These are placed on parcan stand on either side of the stage at a distance to get proper angle to cover the whole stage area. They can also be dimmed as per your requirement to create the mood required on stage. These cost the same as LED Pars. You would generally need at least 16–20 Parcans for a basic event like a seminar, conference, etc.

Focus Light: Focus light is quite strong in its intensity and is usually kept quite far from the stage otherwise the person on stage has no visibility of the audience once the focus is on him/her. The focus light is used more when the venue lights are dimmed and there needs to be attention towards one or few people on or off the stage. This light can be reduced or increased in its coverage area as per the need.

Mics: There are various types of mics that you might need at an event. Stand mics, collar mics, cordless mics, hanging mics, podium mics, and more. All these mics have their own usage depending on the event. However, you should always have a minimum of two mics with cord and two cordless ones. Rest depends on your event's requirements. Please ensure all the mics have fresh batteries in them before the event starts.

Sound Set-Up: Generally, a sound set-up needs a Public Address (PA) system with a laptop and a CD/ DVD player, and speakers of course. The quality of speakers you use will depend on the type of event and your budget. Needless to say, the more you spend the better sound quality you get. But unless it is a music event or a live performance, using very high quality speakers will be a waste of money. For product launches, seminars, conferences, a basic PA set-up works fine. The laptop and DVD player can be used to play videos or audios as per the programme requirement. Another thing that you should keep in mind is that there is no echo at the venue. If you realize that the venue has echo issues, please inform the authorities in advance so that there could be last minute changes in the venue, in that case.

Light Set-Up: Light set-up will have all the lights mentioned above, plus any more lights needed. There are many more lights that can bring different types of effects at the venue. All these will be controlled by a light control panel with an operator. He will need to be guided during your dry run to use these lights as per the flow of the programme.

Other elements: Generally, the sound/light operator will also be able to operate smoke, boosters, confetti, etc. placed on the stage for use whenever required. There must be a fire brigade outside the event venue, in case of an outdoor event with a large number of guests. There should be a generator on standby in case electricity is cut, depending on the scale of the event. Some event organizers do not depend on the electricity and run the whole event with generators to avoid any discontinuity in the event. It is important during live performances to not disturb the flow of the performance and the mood set between the artiste and audience. The set-up may require octanorm stalls in case of exhibitions, food courts, AC structures, ramps, and more, based on the event type. Octanorm stalls are made using boards of 8 ft (h) x 1 mtr (w). General stall size is 3 mtr (l) x 2 mtr (w).

Green Rooms: These are required in case of a live performance involving artistes or a fashion show involving models for make-up and changing clothes. These also give some 'Me-time' to the artistes before the show, during breaks and after the show, to relax. Please ensure the green rooms are clean, comfortable, well-lit, with drinking water and other toiletries stocked up for the artiste. Have a person allocated outside green rooms to take care of any artiste requirements or coordination. These are also used for press co-ordination/interviews before or after the event.

Décor: Any other specific decoration for the event like flower décor, candles, paper material, inflatables, human clowns or cartoon characters, etc.

Manpower

Artistes: Artistes will be part of your event in case of a live performance. They will generally be the biggest part of your cost sheet elements and will have their own specifications and requirements. The technical requirements of artistes are called a 'Tech Rider' and you should have this document to have your light/sound set-up as per the artiste/team. The tech rider can have more details in case of a play or a live show or a dance crew or any other specific performance. Artistes are very specific about their tech riders and, hence, you should be twice as careful with your arrangements for the same. Clarify all doubts before the event to avoid any stressful situations during live event.

Anchor/Emcees: This is the most important front facing

person for your event. So, never cut costs in hiring a professional 'Emcee'. It is an emcee that holds the whole event together and doesn't let audience know of the hassle that's going on backstage. Appearance, clarity of speech, intonations, accent, personality, friendliness and crowd engagement are few of the qualities you should look for in an emcee. Male or female, or both, the choice is yours. Just ensure you check their videos and meet them in person before finalizing them as the emcee for your event. On the day of the event, emcees should be present at the venue at least 3 hours in advance and have a dry run with all the production team in place with the complete set-up ready. Generally, there should be two dry runs completing each activity planned in the event flow so that everyone involved is completely on the same page and remembers all clues. Emcee's fee can range from ₹5,000 to ₹100,000 or more depending on who he/she is.

Event Crew: For a slightly larger event, you will always need a lot of hands to do the running around and manage the operations. This is done by your event crew. You can either hire these from an event manpower agency or hire interns from an event management college on project basis. The crew will handle ticket counters, crowd management, seating arrangements, security arrangements, backstage coordination and more. Crew is generally paid ₹300 per day or more based on your negotiations and amount of work required per day.

Hosts/Hostesses: The other front-facing part of your event manpower are the well-dressed and well-spoken hosts/hostesses. They will primarily be involved in crowd interactions and on-stage work during awards, games, passing mic among the audience during interaction rounds, etc. During an exhibition, they will be required to bring people to your stall. They should reach the venue at least 2 hours before the scheduled time to be able to get briefed properly and also participate in at least one dry run to get a clearer picture of their work. If you find that hosts/hostesses are not performing their duties as per the expectation shared with them earlier (and this will generally happen), please feel free to cut their fee payment for the same, post event.

Photographer: You would always need a photographer for your events, to keep a record of the various moments of the event which can be later shared with the guests as a follow-up activity. These are also useful for your monthly, quarterly newsletters and other internal/external communication later. You need to ensure you share the event flow with the photographer and show him the key people who need to be covered during the event. He should reach the venue at least one hour before the event starts.

Videographer: Videographer is required in case you want to record the event. For seminars and conferences, you do not need permissions from the guests on stage but for live performances, you need permission from the artiste. You cannot officially share this recording on a public platform without permission from people in it. So, please be careful where you use the recorded videos. Having a videographer helps in two ways: to have a live feed on the projector screen during the event; and to have a recorded copy with you post the event. Please ensure your event seating is planned as per the videographer stand, since he/she usually stands right at the centre of the venue and obstructs visibility for people behind him. He/she should reach 2 hours before the scheduled time and be a part of at least one dry run. Their presence is important for the operator to plan switching between the live feed and the laptop screen.

Production Boys: There will usually be production team handling various instruments used during the set-up. These are usually very hard working fellows and a little attention and pat on their back from you will be great.

Other Manpower: These could be need-based manpower like models, butlers, bartenders, fire jugglers, dance performers, etc. The cost for these differs in a wide range. You can negotiate as per your budget.

Licences and Permissions

Any event involving music or live performance or liquor or external event venue needs various permissions and licences in place. IPRS, PPL, fire brigade, traffic police, liquor, etc. are the kind of licences/permissions that you need to take for your event.

IPRS is Indian Performing Right Society and is the sole authorized body in India to issue licences permitting usage of music. This is primarily required in case of any live performances. Basic function of IPRS is to collect royalties on behalf of various artistes involved in the making of that music used by event organizers and distribute it amongst the artistes, music directors, etc. after deducting administrative charges. (Refer to www.iprs.org for more.)

PPL is short for Phonographic Performance Ltd. This licence is required if you plan to play any form of recorded music at your event in public or for commercial purpose. The basic function of this is also to share royalties with the performer and other record company members. You will need this licence in case of DJ based events or any other events where recorded music is played for performances or dance or in the background as well. For more, visit www.pplindia.org.

In case, your event venue is a five-star hotel or a known banquet, it will already have yearly licences/ permissions for itself and you don't need to worry about any permissions. But, you should always check with them while planning and not assume anything. For other venues, these licences are available for a one-day basis too. You will need to get in touch with a person who deals with these legalities or ask your event agency to arrange for the same. However, please ensure you get into the details of the same in your hand and not trust your agency blind-folded. If your event is not ticketed, the fee for licences will be lesser. For a ticketed event, you will need to specify the pricing and quantity of tickets you intend to sell.

Travel and Stay

In case of outstation participants/guests/artistes, you will need to ensure cost for their travel and stay as part of your cost sheet. You can always crack deals with these service providers and involve them as associate partners to save cost. You could provide them logo presence in all marketing communication.

Event Marketing

This depends on whether your event is ticketed or non-ticketed, whether it is an internal event or an external event, etc. If it's a ticketed event with sponsors, you must ensure you utilize all marketing mediums to paint the city with whatever your event colour is! The sponsors need to see their value for money and you will need to very quantitatively provide them the value for their money by giving them branding space, logo presence, offer them titles like powered by or associate sponsors, special sponsorships, on-stage mentions by the emcee and event organizers, AV showcase, free passes, PR coverage, photo-op background, interviews, and much more based on the scale of the event.

You will need a ticketing partner complemented by a powerful online/offline campaign. Even if the event is free, you must do most of these things except that the audience will not have any expectations from you. Sponsors will still have their expectations on value for money.

In case of an internal event, you might still want to do some internal branding like standees, backdrops, signage, presentation slides on projector, etc. Plus, invitations.

In short, you will need to apply almost everything you will learn through this book for your event's marketing too.

Miscellaneous

This head will include managing all kinds of expenses ranging from transportation to food to ironing of clothes, water bottles, tips, other cash expenses made with or without bill and more. Basically, those small expenses which cannot be accounted as separate heads and are dealt in cash with bills produced for the same.

Formats

Following are the formats that will come handy for you during your event planning.

EVENT FLOW

Time	Particulars	Details/Key Responsible Persons	Duration	Special Comments/ Instructions
7.00 p.m.	Event Starts	Emcee comes on the stage and starts audience engagement.	2 minutes	Slide 1 on the screen

7.02–7.10 p.m.	Audience Engagement	Emcee engages with the audience with various questions and other activities.	8 minutes	Live feed
7.10–7.12 p.m.	Introduction to the event and the theme	Emcee introduces the event theme to audience.	2 minutes	Slide 2 on the screen
7.12–7.15 p.m.	Lamp lighting	Emcee invites XYZ for lamp lighting.	3 minutes	Live feed

...and so on.

EVENT COSTING

SAMPLE COST SHEET - << Event Name >>			
Event:	Event Name		
Dates:	<< Event Dates >>		
No. of Days:	X Days		
Sr. No.	**Head**	**Estimates (₹)**	**Actual (₹)**
	Revenue		
1	Targeted Number of Tickets Sold	n	
	[Average Price]	p	
	Tax	v	

2	Rental Income (if any from Space on Hire [SOH])	r	
3	Ticket Sales	= n X (p + v)	
4	**Sponsorship Income** (Final Amount Expected)		
	1. Presenting Sponsor (2) - [₹S1]	S	
	2. Platinum Sponsor (3) - [₹S2]		
	3 Gold Sponsor (5) - [₹S3]		
	4. Silver Sponsor (6) - [₹S4]		
	Total Sponsorships (Inclusive Service Tax)		
	Total Revenues	**TOTAL**	**TOTAL**
	Expenses for Event		
	Elements	Estimated (₹)	Actuals
	SET-UP		
1	Stage		
2	Carpet		
3	Stall/Super Structure		
a)	*Air Conditioning*		
b)	*Food Court set up*		
c)	*Toilets/Handwash*		

4	Podium/ Facia Names		
5	Backdrop		
6	Projector and Screens		
7	Sound Set-Up		
a)	*Mics*		
b)	*Speakers*		
c)	*PA System/Laptop/ DVD Player/Music*		
8	Light Set-Up		
a)	*LED Pars*		
b)	*Parcans*		
c)	*Focus Lights*		
d)	*Other Lights*		
e)	*Lights controller*		
9	Other Set-Up Elements		
a)	*Tables*		
b)	*Chairs*		
c)	*Other element 1*		
d)	*Other element 2*		
10	Green Rooms Set-Up		
11	Décor		
	MANPOWER		
12	Artiste/Performer/ Speaker/Coach		

13	Emcee		
14	Crew		
15	Hosts/Hostesses		
16	Photographer		
17	Videographer		
18	Production Team		
19	Other Manpower		
a)	*Butlers*		
b)	*Bartenders*		
c)	*Other Manpower 1 (e.g. Security)*		
d)	*Other Manpower 2 (e.g. Housekeeping)*		
20	Licences and Permissions		
	TRAVEL AND STAY		
21	For Chief Guest		
22	For Artiste		
23	For Participants		
24	Travel & Stay 1		
	EVENT MARKETING		
25	Hoarding Campaign		
26	Print Ads		
a)	*Ad 1*		
b)	*Ad 2*		
27	Paper Inserts		

28	Radio Campaign		
29	Entertainment Ads		
a)	Entertainment Ad 1		
b)	Entertainment Ad 2		
30	Digital Media Budget		
31	PR/Agencies (in-house)		
32	Miscellaneous		
Total Event Expenses		**TOTAL**	**TOTAL**
33	**Contingency @ 10%**		
	TOTAL EXPENSES		

Terms and Conditions:

1) Service Tax or VAT or GST when applicable will be charged additional to the above total
2) Advance Payment of 'so much' % will be necessary to book the event agency and the team

(Any other terms and conditions may be added here).

Event Checklist

There is no fixed format for this but you must make one for yourself. There are many mobile applications these days which you may explore and use for the purpose. Event checklist is the document which will have each and every requirement for the event listed like a final checklist before the event goes live. You need to ensure that you have one checklist that you keep with you all the time during event preparation and keep ticking elements that are completed and are ready for the event. This will help you not be dependent on your memory all the time and make some better use of your mind space.

EXECUTION

1. Get internal clarity on what exactly you want to achieve as part of this event and what will your requirements broadly be.
2. Invite 3–5 event agencies and give them a brief. Discuss other details or ideas with them.
3. Ask these agencies to share their quotation with you in the event costing format above, with cost details of every element to be used. Ask them specifically that you do not want cost per header like set-up, travel, etc.
4. Once the agencies understand the brief clearly and discuss internally, they work on it and share themes and costing for the event with all requirements and their respective cost.
5. Agencies generally put a 15 per cent agency fee on the top of final cost of all the elements. Ideally, it's not a good idea to negotiate on that bit.
6. However, you should negotiate well on each element and its cost. Most of the agencies keep a

30–40 per cent margin on these elements. So, keep your mind active and wear your negotiation hat on.

7. Once you receive all the quotes, choose top three agencies that you would like to negotiate with and finalize the work with them.
8. Most of the event agencies ask for a 50 per cent advance to be able to start working on the project. That is completely your personal call, along with the interest of company policies. You can ask them to work without advance also, as part of your negotiation session. Or provide a lesser advance too.
9. Once an event agency is finalized based on their fee and advance payment formalities, please brief your ad agency for all the collaterals you need for the event so that they can share design ideas with you for approval and adapt them for various collaterals later.
10. Also, prepare a media plan towards marketing of the event and brief your ad agency for the same too.
11. You might have to coordinate with various participating brands/sponsors for their logo presence on these collaterals before printing or submitting for advertisements.

12. For a ticketed event, you will need to coordinate with various venues apart from online ticketing partner for ticket sales/posters, etc.
13. Once you are closer to the event, please connect with your event agency to ensure they are ready with all the requirements.
14. Usually the event agency would do the set-up a night before the event or throughout the night to have it ready by morning for a dry run, sound check, etc.
15. Handover a copy of the Event Flow to everyone involved in execution of the event.
16. Once the set-up is ready, please have a very strict dry run with all manpower present, running the show as if it is watched by the audience with everything happening to its perfection.
17. Do another dry run. This time without any breaks in explaining stuff to people.
18. Just before the event is about to begin, find your 10 minutes of solace and peace. Freshen up, get ready and refresh your mind from all the stress and tension.
19. Keep calm during the event. Try staying next to the sound console and keep supervising all the operators for execution as per the event flow.
20. Once the event is over, please remember to thank

everyone involved personally and only say positive things. No negative feedback right after the event to anyone. Let everyone enjoy the positive energy of completing something successfully unless there was a blunder clearly visible to the audience.

21. Have a feedback session with everyone involved, the next day, to point out key learnings from the event and how things can be even better the next time.

chapter sixteen

Planning and Executing Activations

The events and activations are usually handled or managed by the same person in a corporate structure. However, I have taken these topics separately since there is a basic difference between the two and you might choose to utilize them at separate occasions based on the returns expected.

Usually, an event is where your brand gets the mileage but customer rarely interacts one-on-one with the product or encounters a representative from your firm. Events will generally involve a lot of branding and less of marketing. However, activation is a perfect tool for marketing. At activations, a potential customer usually gets in direct touch with the product or service or a company representative.

There are several examples of activation: a person

standing near an ATM asking you to apply for a credit card, a newly launched car/bike displayed at a mall for you to check out giving a lead to sales representative present there, a small desk set up at a society with an umbrella shaped branded gazebo (small pavilion) and a company representative sitting there waiting for you to approach him and talk about the product/ service offered, road shows with flyer distribution, and much more.

The cost sheet for activations can be of the same format as for the event. However, your ROMI or objectives may vary as one or more from the ones mentioned below:

Reach: Some activations are conducted only to be able to create higher brand presence and have higher reach for the product/service and its promotion. These could be road shows, branded vans with promoters distributing flyers in key areas in the city, flash mobs[1] in a marketplace or a mall and so on. These types of activations do not involve a longer one-on-one interaction with potential customers. The various photo ops present at multiplex with various movie characters, is also a form of brand activation to increase reach.

---

[1]See: https://en.wikipedia.org/wiki/Flash_mob

Lead Generation: These types of activations are more focused and create data for your organization. When you are approached by a boy at a petrol pump asking for your name, email ID and number to win a gift, it's lead generation. When you go to a nightclub, a photographer clicks your pictures and asks for your contact details to send you those pictures, he is generating leads for himself or for the club. When you go to societies and distribute discount coupons which can be availed at your store in exchange for contact details, you are generating leads. There are various such ways of activations through which you can generate leads for your business. These are extremely important since you could establish a long-term relationship with these leads now. Sooner or later, most of them will convert.

Product/Service Experience: Sometimes when you enter a mall, you see a small kiosk offering free make-up or a free haircut to you. When you enter a multiplex, at times you see a small kiosk with a big LCD/LED TV and a sales representative next to it. Sometimes while entering a club, you will come across promoters offering you free shots of a new drink or free cigarettes. When you go to a fitness event like zumba, capoeira, etc. you might see promoters offering free energy drinks to the guests. These all are examples of activations where the potential customers are given an opportunity to experience the product along with brand promotion. You can plan this for your products and take the cost under marketing budget.

Please do not think that the above aren't intermingled. They are! For example: if a potential customer is experiencing your product, you are also reaching out to a new customer and can also create a new lead by taking his details, if you wish to. So, it all depends on what are you trying to achieve through your activations campaign.

EXECUTION

1. First things first, you will need to decide which type of activation you want to plan. If it is for 'reach', you can look at society activations, road shows, street plays, branded vans, etc. And if it's for lead generation or product experience, you can plan a campaign accordingly.
2. Then you decide on the locations or areas you would like the campaign to cover. There are companies like telecom giants which plan even up to 500–1,000 activations across the country in a span of one month. On the other hand, a real estate player or a mall or a local store could plan

1 or 2 activations over a weekend. So, the choice of locations depends on the kind of campaign you want to start.

3. Next, you have to decide whether to execute the campaign internally with the help of your own team or hire an external agency to help you. There are many event agencies that focus only on activations. You can connect with them and ask for quotations.
4. Another major part of activations is 'permissions'. Whether you are planning society activation or a mall activity or a road show or a branded van activity or anything else, you will generally need to take permissions either from the society office or mall management or traffic police depending on the activity planned. And, if you are planning a national level campaign, you can imagine the level of coordination this will require. For such campaigns, activation agencies come in handy as an additional arm to help you. Generally, event agencies do activations as well. However, there are agencies focusing only on activations and it helps to get your work done by them.
5. Another important part of activations is the collaterals required for the same. For every venue, you will need a set-up and collaterals. These could

be branded canopies, branded table/chair, kiosk, flyers, branded t-shirts/caps, and more. Please ensure you have a complete list of required collaterals ready and you brief your ad agency in advance for the same. Once the designs are ready, it will again be the headache of your activations agency to get them printed and used during the activity. Cost of these should be included in the cost sheet at the time of negotiations.

6. Once activations start, please take surprise visits in various areas and ensure the activity is happening as planned and all the manpower involved knows what they are doing.
7. There should be a daily reporting by your agency covering all the activities conducted and the number of leads generated or contact details collected.
8. The promoters/hosts/hostesses should be paid fixed + variable based on their performance during the day. Targets could also be a factor in calculating the variable part for the payments.
9. Once the activation is over, please ensure you go through all the data collected for its authenticity and keep it safe. Also, analyse it for better understanding of how your campaign did and what can you learn from this campaign that can

be improved in the next one. Add the contact data to your mailing list if possible, to stay connected with all of them.

Event management and activations is a cumbersome job and that's the reason big companies usually have a separate person for events and activations reporting to the marketing manager or head.

chapter seventeen

Planning and Executing Digital Marketing Campaigns

This is one of my favourite topics! I might write my next book on digital marketing and how to utilize it for your brand/product/service. Of course it depends on how you like this book.

Well, digital marketing is the latest in-thing in the market and everyone wants to understand it better, and exploit it to the optimum. There is a paradigm shift in the way marketers today are looking at digital part of their budgets; they are ready to spend on digital marketing and promotions. However, I would like to point out that you should not learn about digital marketing because everyone is doing that. You should learn it because digitization is the future. In times to come, the way we will look at things is going to completely change due to the way our society and work culture is getting completely inclined to digitization. As a marketer, it is already a necessity for you to understand this medium, not just superficially but from the core.

The thing about digital world is that it is accessible to everyone but not everyone is that technology-friendly to be able to understand it. Hence, there is a possibility of various digital agencies taking advantage of your lack of knowledge and charging you more for less or doing less than what is possible. So, this chapter is extremely important for you to understand the basics of digital marketing.

In this chapter, we touch up on certain basics of digital marketing and focus on how to manage your digital agency. I will not be able to train you in using all digital marketing tools and how to use them in this book since that will require a lot of space or a separate book.

Digital marketing for me is the platform that allows you to take your brand/product/service to users who spend time online surfing through the Internet or on various social media websites. Here are a few jargons you need to understand to know digital marketing better.

SEO: Search Engine Optimization is the process of improving your website or blog's position when a search engine shows results for a certain keyword. There are various search engines like Google, Yahoo, Bing, Yandex and more. All of them have different parameters of showing search results. However, the basic criteria are website SEO and off-page SEO.

Website SEO includes usage of relevant keywords in page names, page descriptions, header tags, website content, site links, etc. These are points that need to be considered while developing a website and while managing content of a website.

Off-page SEO includes blogging about the website/business and its products/services, writing articles about the website, creating as many back links as possible for your website, social media, and more. This process takes a lot of time and, hence, off-page SEO results should not be expected before 4–6 months of starting the process. Also, this process should never be stopped till you are actively involved in that business.

SEM: Search Engine Marketing is your substitute till you achieve an organic top position in search engines via SEO. Since SEO takes time to give results, marketers take help of Search and Display ads through Google Display and Search Network to show your ad/

brand to internet users searching for related keywords or visiting websites with related content. These are none other than the same ads that you see above your search results on Google or the ads that you see while visiting various public websites. Even those ads that follow you everywhere on the internet after you visit an e-commerce site. This is primarily achieved through Google AdWords (an online marketing tool by Google) and you can search for it on Google and YouTube and start learning by yourself. Same ads can be created using Bing tools as well. The interface is almost the same as Google AdWords.

SMM: Social Media Marketing is the other big thing that has happened to all the marketers of recent times. With the rise of social media like Facebook, Twitter, LinkedIn, Instagram, Google+, Pinterest, Snapchat, and others, the world has suddenly become a different place for everyone. While users are exploring various fun and social options on these sites, marketers are busy figuring out how to utilize this opportunity to reach out to targeted set of internet users. Every social media platform has internet marketing methodologies. To name a few from Facebook, we have promote post, promote page, display ads, carousel ads, promote website, showcase your products, promote event, app installations, etc. LinkedIn has its own business centric marketing solutions and the same for Instagram or Twitter. Pinterest doesn't have paid marketing features for India, yet. You need to figure at least two of these mediums, to start with, where you would promote your business.

Mobile Marketing: Most of the aspects of mobile marketing are covered via Google Adwords, since there is an option in it while creating a campaign to extend your ads to Google's mobile network as well. However, you can always approach various mobile networks or OEMs (Original Equipment Manufacturers) and have a promotional tie-up for your brand.

- SMS and MMS is still one of the preferred ways for mobile marketing. With the advent of Whatsapp/Snapchat, etc. applications, marketers are trying to attain marketing benefits but no constructive fearless approach—utilizing their enormous database of users worldwide for push marketing—has come out as yet.
- Other important utilization is with bluetooth push messages to mobile phones around a particular transmitter. This transmitter can share various promotional or infomercial

messages with users in its vicinity if their mobile phone's bluetooth is on.

- Another great way to reach out to mobile users is via advertisements in mobile applications or various in-app purchases to add certain additional features in the app, etc.

Affiliate Marketing: With the onset of e-commerce in India, we have come across this term quite a lot. Affiliate marketing is nothing but a third party sending customers to your website or helping you sell your product/service and getting paid to do so. All the existing e-commerce players like Amazon, Flipkart, Alibaba, and many more have affiliate programmes offering varied range of offers to affiliates. As an affiliate of these websites, you can take any of their product and promote it online (with your ID Code in it). If anyone clicks on this product link and buys that product or any other product from the main website, you get paid incentives. There are many people nowadays who make an amazing living only through affiliate marketing.

Content Marketing: With the advent of internet life there is a constant generation of content online. People writing posts on Facebook or tweeting on Twitter; they are all, either creating content by expressing their feelings online or sharing an existing content with their circle of friends. In the midst of all this, there have emerged many content-based companies that create their own attractive content and also help you create attractive content to insert your brand/ product/service in that content to promote it. It's a bit tricky but today's readers are intelligent enough to understand these things. Still, content marketing is a wonderful tool since it works as per a customer's needs and does not force product/service on everyone.

Referral Marketing: This is usually confused with affiliate marketing. But there is a difference. Affiliate marketing is done for money whereas, referral marketing is done by a third party based on trust or relations. These are website referring customers to your website due to a mutual understanding between the two of you or because of an old relation. This also helps improve your SEO ratings. For example: if you own a restaurant and a food blogger refers your restaurant's website on his blog, without taking any favours from you, then it's a genuine referral.

Analytics: This usually refers to Google Analytics. Digital marketing is nothing without analytics. It is all about data and analysis. You need to have the tracking code for Google Analytics encoded on each and every page of your website to be able to get exact data about each and every customer. Analytics can tell you almost everything about a customer who visited your website except his/her name. This data helps you understand what it is that you are doing right in terms of marketing, and what is it that you are doing wrong. Any digital agency you hire will either place this code on your website or ask for details of your Google Analytics account. Most of the data shown to you in the form of presentations with various graphs, is directly available on Google Analytics. So, please do not get impressed very easily and dig deeper. However, Facebook, LinkedIn, Twitter, etc. have their own analytics and these are shared with you once you start your promotions on these platforms.

Email Marketing: I know you think email marketing is the thing of the past and no one cares about it since the conversion ratio is too low (as low as 1 per cent). On the contrary, email marketing is still one of the most favoured mediums of online marketing if done professionally with an in-depth knowledge of the same. There are people who have made a killing only by mastering their email marketing tactics and reinventing it every time. There is a lot to email marketing than just sending emails to a set of email addresses. You need to create opt-ins, you need to create A/B testing fields, you need to understand the email content strategy and more. You can also have email retargeting done via associating Google Analytics with your email campaign. A/B Testing is done in order to check multiple variants of an ad or landing page or newsletter or any other related elements for performance and to find the best performing solution.

Complete digital marketing for your firm can vary anywhere from ₹50,000 to ₹5,000,000 per month based on the amount of work required.

EXECUTION

1. Firstly, decide on the campaign you would like to run for the month or season or year for your brand/ product/ service. Whether it will be purely digital or all across the media.
2. Based on your monthly budget or yearly contract, decide on the amount you would like to spend on the digital campaign.
3. Brief the digital agency with the campaign idea and request it to come back to you with a digital marketing plan for both Google Display Network (GDN – Google's network of those publishers who have given their permission to Google to place ads on their websites) and Social Media.

4. In case your campaign creatives are ready, share the images as well as open files with the digital agency.
5. The digital agency must share the following with you:
   a. A GDN creative which will be adapted to the other sizes by the agency, if required.
   b. Media plan for the GDN including the keywords focused (in Excel sheet format), reach/impressions expected (number of people who came across your ad while surfing the internet), clicks expected (number of people who will click on your ad and visit your website), cost per impression expected, cost per click expected, total cost for the campaign, type of campaign (keywords-based search campaign, interest-based display campaign, placement-based display campaign or others), areas/locations considered and schedule of the campaign.
   c. Social media posts' creative for approval as per the rules and guidelines of these social media players.
   d. For social media, your agency should share a complete calendar showcasing various activities planned on a daily basis and whether

those will be promoted to reach more people or not. A social media calendar should consist of planned posts every day, promoted post or not, ads planned on social media platforms, page promotions, reward to anyone who likes your page or buys your product online, engagement activities on your page or Twitter handle or profile, festival greetings, offer promotions, store promotions, and much more. The agency should bifurcate the media spend for social media and present to you expected reach, clicks, visits, likes, shares, etc.

e. Respective updates/changes/landing pages on the website.

6. After going through these details, discussing internally and with the digital agency, you can go ahead and approve the final plan.
7. The agency goes ahead and submits these ads online and corrects them in case any changes are suggested by Google or social network or publishers.
8. Most of the times, digital agencies will not do anything to your campaign and focus on other clients till your campaign is running. Finally, it will present you with the campaign details fetched from Google Analytics or social networks. Here is when you need to ask for a daily focus, reporting

and have discussions with the agency.

9. On a daily tracking of your digital campaign, you will realize which keywords are working for your campaign and which are not, which ads are costing you higher and which are not, which areas are responding more to you and which less, visitors from which interest categories are spending more time on your website and which less, and much more! That's the beauty of digital marketing and its analysis.
10. You need to constantly optimize and update your campaign as you learn from it. This kind of behaviour is very rare in most of the digital marketing firms and, hence, you will have to be always on the driver's seat even if you know less about the subject matter in this case.
11. Before the campaign starts, please ensure your agency has set proper goals in your digital analytics account to help you analyse your success/failure from the campaign and better your next campaign.
12. After each campaign, sit with your digital agency, preferably in their office with their whole team, analyse the outcomes of your every digital campaign and compare them with expected outcomes. This will help you learn and improve your digital marketing skills.

Digital marketing is a whole new world all together and there is a lot more we need to cover for your knowledge. However, I hope that these basics will help you understand different aspects of it and will help you coordinate with you digital marketing agency for better results.

chapter eighteen

Analysing Your Marketing Spends

One of the most valuable aspects, we have been referring to in almost all the chapters so far is this one: Marketing Spends. It's a bit tricky as well but nevertheless, it is something you must do to understand how you have performed as a marketer. Did your strategy work? Did your campaign work? Did you think it through? What was the reason for success or failure of the campaign? What are the learnings and what will you repeat or avoid in your future campaigns?

First thing that you will need to do before any kind of analysis is data! Here are a few things that you should look at while collecting data:

1. **Call Centre:** If you have given your call centre

number in your marketing campaign throughout all media channels, please make sure you inform your call centre team to ask this simple question to each and every customer who calls on that number—'How did you come to know about us or our offer? Newspaper ad, hoarding, radio ad, TV ad, online ad, social media post or somewhere else?' Also, try to get customer feedback on the quality of the ad, what did they like about the ad and what they did not, if possible. When did they see the ad, what day and what time of the day?

2. **Helpdesk:** In case, you have not given a call centre number but your store or venue's helpdesk number, please make sure that you brief the helpdesk representatives about the campaign and various offers communicated to the customers. Once that is clear to them, tell them to ask the same set of questions mentioned above to the callers.
3. **Cash Counters:** In case you are a retail chain or in a business where customers walk in to your venue/ office/store, please keep a quick form ready to be filled by every customer who comes to your cash counter after making a purchase. If it is not difficult, you can employ someone at the entry or exit to ensure every visitor fills the form.
4. **Walk-ins:** As a marketer, you are always supposed

to keep track of your customer traffic. Be it walk-ins to a store, table bookings in a restaurant, seat bookings in an entertainment arena, or any other business—it is key to maintain hourly/daily/weekly/monthly/yearly data for the traffic your business is getting.

5. **Sales Figures:** Another key area for data collection is maintenance of sales data on an hourly/weekly/monthly/yearly basis as well. This data can be maintained in a comparative format to help with comparing the same figures. Same should be done with walk-ins data above.
6. **Product Sales Data:** You should have data specific to each product for your business to be able to analyse which products are your 'hero' products and which ones will need more marketing efforts, or which need to be stopped. In case of hotels, this could be the type of rooms. In case of restaurants, the type of dish. In case of consumer durables, this could be a type of product selling like ACs, music systems, TVs and further categories. This data should also be maintained on a daily/weekly/monthly/yearly basis. This will help you spot trends and also allot merchandise space accordingly.
7. **Digital Data:** This would involve all the possible

information on the number of page likes, amount of website traffic, number of times shared, number of engagements on social networks, people talking about you on social media, number of followers, retweets, likes on your LinkedIn page, so on and so forth. Data from the world of digital marketing is immense and needs a separate team to analyse the same in comparison to the mainstream data. A well-maintained daily/weekly/monthly/yearly data, in this case, also helps you compare various campaigns and do a comparative analysis of their success.

8. **Attribution Data:** Attribution model is a recent concept utilized by marketers for giving credit to what would have caused the final sales outcome. The concept has been used by a few softwares available with various digital media agencies that help you in analysis of your marketing campaign. Simple process is that this software creates separate calling codes for separate media vehicles used. So, separate calling code for outdoor media, separate one for print media, separate one for radio, and so on. Although, customers will call on these different numbers (codes) for a discount voucher or a free ticket or whatever you are offering them via your campaign to increase your sales, all these calls fall

on the same system and provide expected gifts to the customers. What happens though is that, the software tracks the media vehicle from where the calls come, through the called number (calling code). This helps the software generate data attributing numbers to each media vehicle and helps us understand which mode worked more for us by calculating cost per call per medium.

9. **Any other:** Based on your specific industry, you might have few more sources to gain more data for analysis of your marketing budgets.

Once the data is available with you, it is completely up to your analytical skills to utilize it to create graphs, charts, etc. and get some logical learnings/ understandings out of it. However, these are few reports/graphs you should try to create as a marketer:

1. Sales versus Marketing Spends (YoY/ MoM/ QoQ)[1]

The most important report for a marketer is this one. Generally, your KRAs are partly linked to this. You should have the reports ready with you that compare your sales performance year on year, month on month, and quarter on quarter. This will help you analyse how the performance was for the same month last year

[1]Year on Year; Month on Month; Quarter on Quarter

or the year before, or the same quarter last year and, of course, performance of this year versus last year.

These reports will give you a clear understanding of how your business is performing on a broader level, what is the path it is taking based on the efforts you have been putting and what can be extrapolated to happen in the coming years, considering you do the exact same things you have been doing until now. Your sales targets will also be increased at least by 10 per cent for every new financial year, unless the extrapolation suggests much more. Sales reports are key to any marketing analysis and you should get yourself extremely well versed with each element of it.

What will excite you is when you plot a graph with sales and corresponding marketing spend with respect to every month or quarter or year (y-axis). This graph will give you a clear picture of how your marketing spends have affected sales and if there is any correlation between the two.

2. Leads versus Marketing Spends (YoY/ MoM)

The data you collect from your call centre and helpdesk will help you generate these reports. You can generate following reports through this data:

a. Total leads/enquiries generated as compared to the total marketing spends. This could also be compared with previous data available for daily/weekly/monthly/yearly basis. This will help you understand how effective your whole marketing campaign has been.

b. Leads generated per media vehicle as compared to the total amount spent on it. This will help you decide on the media vehicles which are more cost effective with regard to generating leads for your business.

c. You can always drill deeper and compare leads generated per media vehicle on a month on month basis to correct the elements you use within that media vehicle (provided the amount spent on the media vehicle is same for both the months). For example: if you have generated x leads through your outdoor media campaign last month and you generated 2x leads through your outdoor media campaign this month, you know that the hoardings or bus panels or whichever outdoor media type you used this month fetches you more results. But that's not enough to take a final call on the media vehicle used, you need more information and that's where the next report comes.

3. Bills Generated versus Media Spends/Media Vehicles Used

This report will compare the data you receive from the cash counter or from your online sales counter, if you are taking a survey from your online customers as well.

1. This will have total number of bills generated or the total number of people who actually made a purchase compared with the total marketing spend. This will help you understand the actual quality footfall you received through your campaign. Also, the conversion ratio of the people you are able to invite through your campaigns. A YoY comparison will give you an idea on whether the number of people your campaign attracted is increasing or decreasing or whether your sales team did (or did not) do a good job in converting them into purchases.

b. If you have specific information from each customer at the cash counter it will be easy for you to figure out which media vehicle bought the most customers and so on. So, you can then take an intelligent call based on these reports and the reports mentioned in above points about media vehicles that are giving you 'Quality Leads' (customers who are not only visiting but also buying), and which ones are giving leads that are of no use to the business. If you look properly, you may discover that one media vehicle that was giving you a lot of traffic and had become your favourite, is no longer providing customers who purchase. This will help you rethink your strategy accordingly. A marketer needs to be very careful in analyzing data and no data should be looked in isolation because their meanings often change once data is cross analysed.

4. Footfall versus Media Vehicles/Marketing Spends

The footfall data received from the security persons with 'counters' or with the operations team for your business gives two more reports to you as a marketer:

a. Total footfall compared to the total marketing spend on daily/weekly/monthly/yearly basis. This will help you analyse the effectiveness of your campaign if your purpose was to increase the number of people visiting your venue/store/office. Looking at data from last week, month or year also tells you how much have you improved vis-à-vis last year or how are days without marketing compared to days with marketing efforts.

b. The other report you can generate here is categorizing the total footfall on the basis of the media vehicle that drove them to your business location. This will help you attribute the success of your campaign to a specific media vehicle and, hence, improve your plans for the next campaign. The attribution data discussed above is also going to help you make this report precise and improve your marketing acumen.

5. Products/SKUs (Stock Keeping Unit) Reports

These reports are necessary to understand which products are working for your business and why. You can create many types of reports related to products depending on your business needs. Few of them are:

a. **Product/Services Units Sold versus Footfall Report**: This report will help you understand which products are most in demand and, hence, maintain your store capacity accordingly. This will also help you understand the category of products that are doing better for your location as compared to the rest of the product/service categories. Further daily/weekly/monthly/yearly comparison of this data will also help you understand your 'Product Life Cycle' and seasonal dependency for better business.

b. **Products Sold versus Media Vehicles Report:** This is a little too much to ask but if you dive deeper and get this data, it will be simply amazing. This report will basically compare people coming via different media vehicles make what kind of purchases. This will be an effective calculator of media vehicles' ROMI, impact and spending capacity of the customers coming through it, for your marketing analysis.

6. Digital Media Reports

One thing that digital marketing will never disappoint you about is the amount of data that it generates for your study and analysis, and the number of reports you can generate from it. In fact, there is too much data available for digital marketing and, hence, it is important to understand which data you want and which one you don't want.

Just to help you understand the amount of information you can get through these reports, here are a few pointers:

a. Is your traffic coming from Google Ads/ organic search/social media/directly or some other way?

b. How many males and how many females are part of the traffic?
c. What is the age group of this traffic?
d. Which location is the traffic coming from?
e. What are the interest levels of people visiting your website?
f. What is the traffic doing after reaching your website?
g. Which device are your visitors accessing your website from?
h. Which operating system or web browser are your visitors using?
i. What is the percentage of users who are not doing anything on your site and leaving?
j. How many visitors are performing a relevant task while they are on your site like going through content for long, downloading documents, watching videos, filling forms, signing up, making a purchase, etc.?

With the help of Google Analytics, you can analyse all the digital data related to your website for the benefit of your current as well as future campaigns.

I hope, this chapter helped you understand that a marketer's job isn't all about glamour as is generally perceived. It's also about the numbers and data crunching. You have to be a master of numbers and good at analysing data to make sense of these reports and devise future strategies.

Yet, a wrong perception most of the times is that if someone can remember numbers better, he is good with numbers. Please be very clear that remembering numbers and playing with numbers are two different things, and should never be confused with each other. A person can be bad at memorizing numbers or keeping them in his conscious mind to flaunt them during meetings, but that doesn't make him a great data analyser. You should be able to derive a story out of raw data—that's a skill!

Please start playing with numbers and deriving various types of graphs and pie charts from them to master the art of data analytics. If you are able to draw out top 5–10 business inferences from the data provided to you, then you are good. No need to remember the numbers behind these inferences if you can't.

Just make sure you get the learnings right. Rest of the data can always be referred to through Excel sheets and your brain doesn't need to be worried about it, if that's not you. Like they say about Einstein, he was extremely poor with his memory and could never remember dates, phone numbers, etc. But he went on to become the greatest physicist of all time.

chapter nineteen

What is 'Negotiations' for Me as a Marketer?

As a teenager, and even later as a young marketing professional, I used to hate people who would negotiate. I used to think very low of them. Wherever they went shopping they would start negotiating—be it vegetable market or an apparel store or a consumer durables market or while buying grocery, and more.

I used to think why do people haggle so much only to save a few bucks which is not even of such big value to them. But, soon after, I realized that being a negotiator is not situational, it's a habit. And, you need to inculcate it in you irrespective of whichever profession you are in. People who negotiate with vegetable-sellers, don't do it as much to save a few bucks as much they do it for the fun of negotiating. And, once you start doing it, it becomes your acquired skill. It will only get better and better with practice, especially in your work environment, as a marketer.

When I started my career as a hardcore marketer at Peninsula Land Limited, it was also a 180 degree shift in my career since I was on the other side of the table then. Before Peninsula happened, I was on the vendor side, be it outdoor media or business consulting or event management. So it was extremely challenging for me to negotiate with various vendors initially, as a marketer. I was not able to crack amazing deals and my boss would always be unhappy with me due to the same. My negotiation skills became a major concern to my bosses. However, thankfully they understood the fact that it's primarily because I have come from the other side of the table and, hence, get a bit emotional towards the vendors while we try to arm twist the lowest quotes from them. They gave me a fair time to build this skill and also nominated me for various negotiation skills-related trainings that were offered by our corporate HR.

Due to the amount of work I was handling, I was also given a junior resource—a Gujarati girl. This was the aha! moment of my marketing career, specific to learning the art of negotiation. I would take her along with me on recce to various cities for selecting billboards for our outdoor media campaigns, and even without having any industry knowledge of hoarding rates, she would start negotiating with the vendor after the recce. I was amazed to see the confidence in this young girl when she used to negotiate. Of course I realized that this comes as a trait in most of the Gujaratis since they mostly belong to business families and learn these ropes since their childhood. Here are a few ground rules that I grasped during my learning phase, and I am sure they will do you some good too:

1. Keep your heart/emotions aside while on the negotiating table. A negotiation means business and there is no room for someone who can get emotional for the other side.
2. Be calculative and do not be in a hurry to close the deal, even if you are too desperate from inside. Do not show your desperation or restlessness in any way to the other side.
3. Don't think twice while giving the first offer. How much ever idiotic or illogical it may sound in the first go, whatever the other side quotes, be straight forward and offer them up to 50–60 per cent of the amount, very strongly, to start with (unless you already know the market rates and want to offer more). This will either make or break the deal but will definitely make the other side unstable giving

you more control while negotiating.

4. However urgent the work may be, always remember that it's you who is going to spend the money. So, you should always try to have the upper hand during the negotiations. Yes, you will reach a win-win deal in the end, but learn to not give in too soon.
5. Always either take long pauses or no pauses at all, before making a counter offer to the other side. This will keep him on his toes and also keep him restless.
6. Always play the wait-and-watch game if you have some time in your hands. If the deal doesn't seem to be getting closed to your comfort point, feel free to tell the other side that you don't think it will work out as simply like that but will take some time to discuss their offer internally and will get back to them. Don't call them for the next 2–3 days and wait for them to call you. Once they call you, offer them whatever best (maximum savings possible) you can and inform them so. Inform them that this is your last offer—take it or leave it. They will generally close the deal at your final offer, in most cases. If not, and if you really need to close the deal urgently, come down a little and close at whatever best rate you can.

7. Another tool for further saving is to request the vendor to include taxes as part of the final amount discussed. Most of the time it will be quite difficult to have this part closed, but you can finally make a lump sum offer of an all-inclusive amount which will be much lesser than basic amount + taxes.
8. Negotiations can sometimes go for up to 2–3 months (sometimes a year or more) depending on the deal size. So, being patient is another extremely important requirement for best negotiations to happen.
9. Always make sure, you enjoy negotiations. On the negotiation table, there are no friends, no relatives, no acquaintances. It is plain and simple business. Both parties are representing their respective companies and there is nothing personal.
10. Your most important friend during all work-related negotiations is the representative from your company's commercials department. Please ensure you have a good tuning with him to be able to play good cop/bad cop whenever required to manage vendors and deal closures.

Money saved is money earned! Keep track of all these instances of negotiations that you have done to save company's money and make a note of the total amount saved by you. Present it to your bosses at the time of your appraisal to quantitatively present your efforts as a marketer.

While negotiating for cost, please make sure the focus on the quality expected does not go away and you ensure best possible quality in the best possible cost. Negotiations will be very important to you throughout your career as a marketer or an entrepreneur. In fact, one of the KRAs for marketers is the percentage of marketing budget saved during a financial year.

Negotiations may not always involve money. In case of tie-ups and mergers, negotiations are in kind or over authority or many other things. However, the rules of engagement do not change much. So, go out there and always try to get the best (the least) cost for yourself, your home, your company and your people.

Good luck with negotiations!

chapter twenty

Selecting Vendors

As a marketer, a lot of your time will go into managing existing vendors or selecting new vendors. Most of the companies, these days, have a policy of getting at least three quotations for a new job that needs to be completed. The basic reason being 'market correction' of the rates you are paying your existing vendors and also factual reference while negotiating to close the job.

So, there would be two kinds of agencies/ vendors helping you: first, the strategic, ideation, conceptualization, creative or online presence side of the business; and second would be the vendors supporting you on the execution side of the business. Maintaining a balance between these two is very crucial and comes as you grow as a marketer. Following are various types of vendors (who are usually not on an annual retainer basis) you will most probably deal with as a marketer:

1. Newspaper Distribution Agencies

These are the vendors helpful to you when you want to do a flyer inserts distribution campaign for marketing your latest offers or products or event. These agencies have an enormous distribution system throughout the city and can help you reach out to your potential customers on the basis of the areas covered. You can discuss with the vendor which newspaper, area, dates, etc. you want to schedule your inserts to suit your overall plan and they will execute it accordingly. You should try and keep at least 2–3 of these vendors empanelled with your commercials department to be able to negotiate best rates. Empanelment of vendors would include calling various vendors for your regular work to office, giving them a brief on the kind of work that is usually required and asking them to submit their best rates for that work. These rates are then further negotiated based on the quantity of work expected and your negotiation skills with vendors. Once empanelled, you do not need three quotes every time you take help from any of these vendors. This also helps you save a lot of cost.

2. Offset Printing Vendors

One of the most crucial vendor for you is the vendor that supplies printed flex, vinyl, sun board, and other marketing/branding material and mounts it wherever required. This is the most regular work for a marketer in almost all the industries. Flex will be required for your outdoor media campaign, your store branding, your events, your external branding panels, poles and what not. This will also be your vendor whose staff will work day and night for you to keep things ready before the deadline or a launch or a campaign or a festival or a show and so on.

These vendors should also be empanelled with most of the rates fixed as the same for all the vendors. Work should be given to all in a circulated manner to keep everyone involved and on their toes. Giving all work to one vendor will spoil that vendor and he might start taking you for granted. And the other vendors will not take you seriously since you do not give them a lot of work. Your work can be on low priority for them as compared to their existing clients. Also, negotiating with them can become a pain.

3. Paper Printing Vendors

There will be hundreds of collaterals you will need to be printed on different types of papers. Flyers, calendars, posters, danglers, table tops, offer booklets, newsletters, annual diaries, office branded stationary, books, presentations, pitches, and more. Always have at least three of these vendors empanelled with your organization to be able to divide work at the time of urgency and also take advantage of the best quality output of various vendors depending on the product.

4. Fabrication Vendors

As a marketer you will be constantly involved in building various branding collaterals to be used at various occasions. These could be branded panels of MS frames or acrylic letter cuts for your logo, back-lit stainless steel communication (letter/logo frame made with flat and wide stainless steel rods with LED lights fixed behind them to reflect light from the wall on which the frame is mounted), or grazing of glasses to give brand communication at office or stores, creation of direction boards, pylons, wall graphics, and much more. These are the vendors who specialize in metals, welding, lighting, etc. related work and have good knowledge of various products in these areas. You should have more than 3 such vendors listed with you to receive quotes for the work immediately. No need to empanel them since this is not going to be a regular work. However, the rates quoted by these vendors for the same work may vary a lot. This is due to the difference in the material they use to complete the work.

There may be a vendor quoting higher but he may also be using high quality material. So, while receiving quotes from these vendors, please ask them to give each and every detail about the materials used. Once quotes are received, sit with your commercials/ accounts person and engineering person to identify the best vendor. Selecting vendor here is going to be the most tricky part. So, please choose wisely.

5. Permissions/Licences related Vendors

As a marketer you might come across situations where you are required to obtain certain permissions to be able to complete a task. It could be a liquor licence for your wine and cheese evening or traffic permissions for a road show. It could be a municipal authority permissions for putting pole kiosks by the side of the roads or getting PPL/IPRS licences for a musical concert at your venue.

Usually, you will have your events and operations teams to assist you with this. However, you should always have the contact numbers of at least 2–3 agents who work in this area to get the situation under control, if a difficult one arises. These are rare occurrences, but it's better to be safe than sorry always.

6. Event Management Agencies

These are listed in this section since these are usually not on a yearly retainer basis with a company and companies like to keep it open for them to choose event agencies based on their events. However, you must have at least 5–6 event agencies on your fingertips who have a good relation with you and will be ready to work with you whatever the urgency of situation maybe. These agencies would also not take benefit of your situation at any stage and, hence, would be very reliable in that sense.

In case of a big event, you might want to utilize multiple agencies to handle various parts of the event to save cost, dependencies and also utilize the best of all. Procure set-up from one, manpower from another and artistes from a third one. All are happy and all will work with you again too.

7. Activations Vendors

These are agencies that find a lot more room to be on a yearly retainer depending on the industry they serve. Usually, telecom and banking sectors have the most regular use for activations and hence they prefer to work with few empanelled agencies at a central level. Regional and local level coordination becomes too much headache for marketers.

However, be it society activations or road shows, be it street plays or mall promotions, a marketer needs an activations agency to do all the hard work or permissions, coordination and delivery. There are various agencies that offer all types of activations under one umbrella and then there are many others which specialize in a certain type of activations. Rural marketing utilizes the maximum of these agencies since that's the easiest way to reach the bottom of the pyramid.

You should have activity/speciality-based activations agencies registered with you to take help on a need basis. Always try to do surprise checks on the way these agencies are performing their task. Due to the kind of manpower coordination involved in large scale activations, the quality of work suffers sometimes. It's important to keep a check on the same.

8. Outdoor Media Vendors

Once again listing these here since they are also not on a retainer basis with a company and are utilized on a need basis. Here, a marketer would be required to know all the outdoor vendors in the city. Outdoor vendors will always offer you their own sites but also other sites which they feel that you might like based on their understanding of you.

But the catch here is that, the sites that they own will be lower in cost as compared to the ones they arrange from other vendors. Hence, it's always advisable for you to ask them to show you only their own media sites. For the owner of any other media sites that you like, you can either push the vendor to share details of the owner company or you can just go near the hoarding and you will find a small plate with the owner's details mentioned on it. Most of the time it works.

So, take hoardings from owners only and negotiate the rates as best as possible. The longer the duration you want the hoardings for, the more you can negotiate. You can also ask the vendors to give you printing/mounting free for the first creative. Plus, make sure he reprints and mounts the creative in case it gets torn due to any natural cause.

9. Corporate Gifting

As a marketer, you will utilize many gifting items to keep and build strong relations with your clients, customers, retailers, or any other stakeholders. This is where you will utilize services of various corporate gifting vendors. These vendors will generally have an online or a PDF copy of their product catalogues which can be branded for your corporate gifting during festive season or anniversary or new year or other special occasions.

You should have more than 4–5 corporate gifting vendors to choose best suitable products for your gifting ideas. Negotiations with these will vary based on your desired quantity but you can always push harder and get the best deal possible.

10. Gift Vouchers

As part of your marketing campaigns, you would like to offer attractive gifts to pull your customers and purchase products/services. These could be ice cream vouchers for two or movie tickets for two, or travel vouchers to national/international destinations to free rides from your travel partner. There are various agencies like Travelport, RewardPort and many more that offer these gift vouchers at almost 5–10 per cent cost of the perceived value based on the bulk orders placed to them and I advise all marketers to utilize these marketing tools for good.

Gift vouchers can be collected either by paying for them or by making tie-ups with respective brands. In either case, these work as a great pull for your campaigns and a marketer should always figure out ways to wow his customers who ensured his campaign achieved its due success.

This is not a concise list of types of vendors and you will find many more industry specific vendors as a marketer. However, I hope I have covered the most frequently used ones here. You will be able to find almost all of the above types of vendors in your city on websites like www.indiamart.com or www.justdial.com, etc. apart from your personal circle and colleagues.

chapter twenty-one

Liaising with Various Agencies

There will be a few agencies which you will need throughout the year to help strategize, plan and execute your marketing efforts. These will generally be on a retainer basis, meaning you will sign a contract with them to avail their services for a period of one year and renew the contract if you are satisfied with their work. In most cases, the agencies on retainer basis will be:

1. PR Agency

There are many PR agencies in India working at national as well as local level. As explained earlier, it's critical for most marketers to have a PR firm working hand-in-hand with them.

PR firms usually charge a fixed monthly fee in case

of a retainer relationship and provide all the services required by your business without any extra bills. However, in case of dinners or drinks with journalists and reporters, separate bills are provided and paid on 'actuals' basis. In most cases, the additional amount spent on PR is quite less compared to the other two agencies, namely ad agency and digital marketing agency. Whereas the results obtained are very solid and long lasting.

2. Ad Agency

This is almost like your right hand, as a marketer. A marketer cannot do anything alone without the support of a good advertising agency. This is the agency that does most of the thinking and creative work for your business. Although yes, their emotional attachment with the client's business is sometimes questionable. They love some of their clients' brands. Whereas, they service some others only to keep their kitchens running.

All your marketing/branding related work you plan will come from them in a soft copy format which will need to be printed or fabricated to ensure smooth execution. These agencies are usually on retainer basis and enjoy heavy monthly fees. Apart from the retainer fee, the bigger part of cash flow with an ad agency is of media spends. All the print and radio media is bought via the ad agency. This is because every accredited agency gets 15 per cent discount for media ad space booking for print/radio/TV as compared to a direct customer. Out of the 15 per cent, an ad agency usually keeps 2–3 per cent and shares the rest of it back with you. You would never get these savings if you were releasing your ads yourself directly with the media house as a policy signed between associations of ad agencies and various media vehicles.

3. Digital Agency

Another extremely important agency that you can also call as your left hand! These are the agencies that help in conceptualizing, planning and executing your digital marketing campaigns. Be it Google Display Network, Search Network or the social network, digital agencies are your partners all the way.

Your digital agency will present to you all that you can do online to promote your brand/product/services. In general, they are supposed to share monthly plan of all digital activities with you in advance and later produce monthly reports along with the bills. These reports should also be discussed in a meeting to understand your ROMI and correct the course in case required. It will not be easy for you to understand a lot of the reports unless you have a knowledge of the field. I suggest you to do a certificate course in digital marketing from any well-known institute in your city or take up an online course.

In some cases, companies have a separate creative house on retainer and issue media releases through a different media buying agency. So, basically, you brief a creative agency to give you a creative for your marketing promotion and share a CorelDRAW or Illustrator file with the media buying agency to release the same with selected media house (print/ TV/radio). The percentage of discount received is almost the same in this case as well. However, the final rate that you get through a media buying agency can be lower than the rate an ad agency gets you. That is because, a media buying agency buys media space in bulk from all media houses for a year at a highly-negotiated rate and, hence, it can extend the benefit of the same to you as well. However, this process needs much more coordination and becomes a hassle for a marketer facing multiple deadlines for multiple media releases or promotional activities.

Agency Selection Process

This is something you will thoroughly enjoy as a marketer! By now you might have already heard of the famous agency selection process conducted by—Nearbuy. If not, do search on Google for a video of the founder of Nearbuy.

In case you are looking for a new agency for any of the above-mentioned profiles or something else too, first thing you will need to do is to find out your options in or around your city. It is suggested to have your agency in the same city in order to reduce communication and understanding gap and have freedom to hold meetings without too much planning and delay. However, in case, you find good tuning with your agency in long-distance as well, it's completely fine to go ahead with that.

The steps that you will have to follow are:

1. First and foremost, you will have to find out at least 5–8 agencies through your own circle, colleagues, seniors or other agencies who are either well-known in their field or are referred by someone known to you. Call all these agencies and brief the concerned person about your business and marketing requirements and your expectations from them. Also, give them an idea about the amount of work they can expect to be delivered per month. So, in case the agency is small and cannot take up the workload expected, they can

withdraw their proposal without wasting their own time and yours.

2. Once all agencies are briefed, fix up a date with the panel of your seniors and colleagues, who will be part of the agency selection process, for agency presentations.
3. Keep one single date for all agency presentations and schedule the timings accordingly. Generally, give at least 15 days' time to agencies so that they can be available on the same date, as per your schedule.
4. Tell all the agencies clearly on what do you expect them to cover in their pitch. They should generally cover their introduction, client list, testimonials, awards, famous campaigns and other generic USPs in the first 5–10 minutes of their presentation. Then they can get on to their understanding of your business, various products/services you offer, current brand and market position you hold and various challenges faced by you at present in the next 5–7 minutes. Rest of the 10–15 minutes should be spent by the agency in explaining how do they see your business differently, what will they bring on the table to help you face those challenges in a better manner and how will they help you increase your business and achieve your

targets as a partner. They can finally end with their organizational culture, relationship management and value system along with the estimated retainer fee and deliverables for the same.

5. After a thirty-minute pitch, you can keep 15 minutes for Q&A with every agency and dive deeper into more relevant areas related to your business requirements and if the agency pitching has worked with any clients from similar industry earlier. You will notice that most of the agencies will come with a minimum of 3 members with differing expertise to showcase their strength and seriousness towards the pitch.
6. If the pitch looks promising, you can also ask for 2 client contacts for reference check that can be done at a later stage.
7. Once the pitches are done for the day, you can have an internal meeting on the same day or the next day to get everyone's views and finalize on an agency to start negotiations with.
8. As usual, the aim of negotiations will be to reduce your final cost for all the work that you will need from the agency.
9. You can also define key parameters and mutually agreed targets to divide the retainer fee into two parts—Fixed and Variable. Fixed is something you

will pay every month and Variable can be paid every quarter or every 6 months or annually based on the target achievement by agency in that time period.

10. Generally, this value can be paid on a pro-rata basis from 80 per cent target achievement to 120 per cent target achievement. So, if the agency achieves 80 per cent or more of the target decided at the start, they will be paid the same percentage of the decided variable fee. The upper limit of payment will be up to 120 per cent of target achievement. Anything above that will be paid 120 per cent of decided variable fee only. At the same time, anything below 80 per cent of target achievement will not be paid anything at all. For example: if your target is ₹100 then a) if your company achieves anything below ₹80 the agency will not get any variable fee b) if your company achieves ₹90 agency will receive 90 per cent of the variable fee c) if your company achieves ₹120 agency will receive 120 per cent of the variable fee amount d) if your company achieves ₹140 agency still gets 120 per cent of the variable amount. So, setting up these metrics in the very beginning is crucial to set expectations right before starting work with the agency.

11. Once finalized, you can arrange for a team visit to the selected agency's office and may be a half a day workshop to brief the agency resources and the client servicing team in more detail about the kind of work they can expect coming from you and the kind of quality of work you would expect from them. This team visit is also important to look at their office and infrastructure apart from the general brief.
12. You should also arrange for a team visit by the ad agency to your business location, factory, mall, project, etc. to give them a feel of what they are working for. It helps them connect better with the work they are going to do.

This should be sufficient for you to be able to start working with the agency. It wouldn't be wrong to expect initial hiccups in dealing with each other. It takes at least 2–3 months for an agency to get used to your style of working and the quality of work expected. That's one of the reasons why most of the corporate companies do not like to change their agencies every year unless left with no other choice.

Agencies also aim towards serving a client for a long time and establishing a stable relationship with them. They also expect the retainer fee to be increased every year to be able to maintain the cost increase due to inflation. Another reason being, they might have quoted quite low in the first place to be able to get your account while pitching. But after proving their worth they would like to ask for a raise to manage their own resource schedules.

Hope this chapter helps you in selecting and coordinating with agencies in a more prepared and better way.

chapter twenty-two

Managing Your Bills and Contracts

This is another non-glamorous and unattractive side of a marketer's job. Managing bills, processing bills, making sure your vendors and agencies get paid on time, creating and maintaining contracts, and more. As boring as it might sound to you, but it is one of the most crucial parts of your job.

As a marketer, please remember that it's extremely important that everyone knows you as an honest and transparent person, especially when it comes to money matters. You should try as strictly as possible to follow company procedures related to vendor or bills or contracts management, not just for your company but also for your own safety in future. Since you would be a part of the only few in your firm whose job is to spend company's money, everyone will at first look at you with a bit of cynicism. Often some marketers get tempted to conduct fraudulent activities to make some quick money apart from their salaries. There are various tactics they use for the same but I am not going to give you a crash course on all that. On the contrary, I suggest you to stay completely away from all those activities as well as such people. And if required, please report such incidents/people to your senior officials, maintaining confidentiality.

Trying to cheat your employer will always make you feel guilty, it will never make you more confident about yourself since you will always live in fear. It will not earn you respect from your vendors and in case of panic situations you will not be able to get aggressive with your vendors and push them harder to finish a task at hand. Moreover, the vendors you try to make your partner in crime would start to talk and gossip about you with your counterparts, successors and predecessors sooner or later. It will slowly spoil your reputation in the market and in the office also. So, a simple suggestion—stay away from unethical practices. Be straight forward and be strong.

Why I took a moment to express the importance of being ethical is because your seriousness towards the contract and bill management will completely depend on how clearly you understand the nature of your work and how easy it will be for others to point a finger at you. Also, as a marketer, please understand the importance of your signature. Your signature on a document carries a lot more weight in your work life than you think. Anything goes wrong with a bill or contract, you will be directly responsible for it. And, in the matters of money, I am sure you know that most of the time situations get ugly. Plus, you lose trust of your seniors too. So, please be extra careful before taking any bills from a vendor and signing on it. Also, while signing please ensure you write the date of the receipt as well. This helps you chase people when payments are delayed and also provides proof of delay internally to put pressure on getting cheques processed for your vendor.

Yes, you can be as strict with your vendors and agencies as you like for your work, but it will always be as limited as your promptness of payments to them as per the contracts. The more you delay payments, more you lose respect and less response you will get. So, you need to follow up internally with your finance department for cheques towards your vendors and agencies. Sometimes put up fights as well since the finance department will find a way or another to delay payments for better cash flow of the company.

Bill Management and Processing

Having mentioned the importance of bill processing above, please follow the following process to manage your bills:

1. Prepare a monthly marketing plan with estimated budget for the upcoming ads, retainers, events, etc. for the next month and share with your seniors for approval by 25th day of the present month.
2. You can use the format shown in table 1 and 2 of chapter 7. This will help you stay organized and have all the info in one place.
   For example: following can be your marketing calendar for the month with approved budgets.
3. As and when you start executing marketing activities in the month and vendors start sending you bills, you can keep filling the 'actuals' column in the following table next to the approved budget amounts.

Table 1

Marketing Calendar for ABC (June, 2017)						
Mon	**Tue**	**Wed**	**Thur**	**Fri**	**Sat**	Sun
			1	2 Flyer Distribution; Radio Ads	3 *Pune Times* (Full Page); Flyer Distribution; Radio Ads	4 Flyer Distribution; Radio Ads
5	6	7	8	9 Flyer Distribution; Radio Ads	10 *Pune Times* (Half Page); Flyer Distribution; Radio Ads	11 *Pune Mirror* (Full Page); Flyer Distribution; Radio Ads
12	13	14	15	16 Flyer Distribution; Radio Ads	17 Medianet (Half Page); Flyer Distribution; Radio Ads	18 Flyer Distribution; Radio Ads
19	20	21	22	23 Flyer Distribution; Radio Ads	24 *Sakaal Times* (Half Page); Flyer Distribution; Radio Ads	25 Flyer Distribution; Radio Ads
26	27	28	29	30		

Table 2

Sr. No.	Marketing Bill Details				
	Particulars		*Budget*	*Actuals*	*Details*
1	Print		**= A + B + C + D + E**	= a+ b + c + d + e	Bifurcation
	a) *Pune Times* (FP)	A			
	b) *Pune Times* (HP)	B			
	c) *Pune Mirror* (FP)	C			
	d) Medianet (HP)	D			
	e) *Sakaal Times* (FP)	E			
2	Radio	F	**= F**	= f	
3	Outdoor		**= G + H**	= G + H	Bifurcation
	a) Pole Kiosks	G			
	b) Direction Boards	H			
4	Digital - Media Spends	I	**= I**	= i	
5	BTL (Distribution)	J	**=J**	= J	

Sr. No.	Marketing Bill Details				
6	Collateral & Production (In Mall Branding + Coupons Printing)		**= K + L + M**	= K + L + M	Bifurcation
	a) Book Printing	K			
	b) Flyer Printing	L			
	c) Branding Collaterals	M			
7	PR	N	**= N**	= n	
8	Events (Event Budget)	O	**= O**	= o	
9	Agency Retainer	P	**= P**	= P	
10	Misc & Gifts	Q	**= Q**	= q	
11	Retailer/ Brand Support	R	**= R**	= r	
		TOTAL	**TOTAL**	**TOTAL**	

**Please note that in the above table, lowercase value for actual amount signifies that usually the final bill that you will receive in these media vehicles will be lower than the budgeted amount due to agency discounts or less expenses than planned. However, the ones with uppercase value for actual amount signifies that the bill received will be of almost the same value or bit higher due to additional taxes.*

4. Before taking the bills from any vendor or agency, make sure you check the bill amounts properly and verify them with the agreed rates. Consult your commercials department counterpart if need be. Also, make sure that the vendor has attached all the work proof documents along with the bill for the finance team to understand and visualize the work completed. These could be as follows:
   a. In case of a print ad bill, it should be attached with a copy of the newspaper page showcasing the advert/insert.
   b. In case of a flex printing and mounting bill, it should have images of all the final mounted media assets.
   c. In case of a flyer, it should be attached with a sample of the flyer.
   d. In case of a magazine ad, bill will need to have a copy of the magazine.
   e. In case of an ad agency retainer, bill will need to have monthly report attached.
   f. In case of a digital agency retainer, bill should have monthly report of the work completed.
   g. In case of media spends on digital, the bill should have a report of media spends and ROMI from that for each online asset used.
   h. In case of radio ads, bill needs to have a

copy of the schedule and then the final sheet mentioning all the actual spot timings for your ad (not in Excel sheet but in the form of an official document).

i. In case of TVCs, you will need schedule copy as well as final spot timings from the channel (not in Excel sheet but in the form of an official document).

So, basically, all bills should have a proof of work attached with them, unless it is an exception where proof cannot be attached. Only then should you take them from your vendor and never in any other case. Do not try to be overly nice with vendors on these matters as these can backfire at you anytime later. Also, never ask your vendor to keep the bills on your desk and that you will check them later or give the bills to any of your colleagues in your absence. It is your work and your responsibility. You must take the bill personally and verify it properly before taking it. A sign saying 'Received' means that you were okay with the bill presented. So, please be careful by not being over-confident or over-trusting any vendor.

5. Once you take the bill and input the 'actual' amount in your marketing sheet, you can use the following format to also maintain details of the bills processed.

Details of Submitted Bills (reference sheet for Finance Team)					
Vendor	Invoice Number	Amount	Handed Over To	Handover Date	Paid On
Vendor A	xxx	a	Accounts	******	
Vendor B	xxx	b	MD's PA	******	
Agency 1	xxx	p	Accounts	******	
Vendor C	xxx	c	PAID	******	

Maintaining this is important because, many a times, you might lose track of the bills that you have received/not received or processed/not processed. This happens quite often if you are managing multiple activities with multiple vendors. Also, at times, you will suddenly hear from the vendor that he has submitted the bill several months ago only to find out from this sheet that he had in fact submitted it only 15 days back. Or hear from the finance team that they have not received the bill only to verify from your sheet the date on which you submitted it. So, being organized is extremely important for a marketer in order to manage the marketing budgets well and also keep track of what is spent and what is left.

6. After filling these details for each bill, please forward the bill for signatures of the respective seniors along with a copy of your marketing sheet with budgeted versus actual figures and submit it to the finance department for further processing.
7. General credit period signed by most of the companies is from 30–45 days. The vendors will start following up with you on payments, if they are not paid within the credit period. In turn, you will have to constantly follow up with your finance team for payments to be released for these vendors or agencies.
8. Once a payment is done and a cheque is released, in most cases, it will be given to you by finance team to hand it over to the respective vendor/agency.
9. As a practice, you should always take a photocopy of the cheque and take a 'received' signature from the person who is collecting the cheque on behalf of the vendor/agency.
10. Go back to your marketing sheet from point 5 above and update the status of the vendor's bill as 'Paid'.

This completes your one cycle of bills management and processing. You will have to repeat this every month as a marketer. So, you can either process the bills as and when they come to you or fix a day of the week when you will take out an hour to process bills received in the last one week. Do not delay processing from your side since everyone else is anyway going to take their own time.

Contract Managment

As a part of your job, you will definitely be involved in discussion, finalization and signing of many contracts. Contracts can be with ad agencies, digital agencies, event management agencies, PR agencies, IT firms, vendors, etc. depending on work requirements.

Well, contracts being contracts, most of them are legal in their language and beyond your quick understanding of the clauses mentioned in them. However, I would suggest you read every contract word by word and try to understand it along with the help of legal resource person in the company. Soon you will understand that all the clauses mentioned in a contract are very logical and important. This will help you understand how contracts work and how to negotiate better with vendors, agencies or partners on various terms and conditions mentioned in the contracts.

General process to do this is to involve a corporate legal person right from the beginning. Make him understand all the discussions and negotiations you have conducted with this agency/vendor before finalizing it for the services it is going to offer to your company. Share supporting documents with him to give him more clarity on vendor's company structure, history, clientele, etc.

After understanding things clearly, he will draft a contract to be shared with the agency. The important areas you should look at in this draft are scope of work, contract term, fee structure, payment policies and exit clause. These are critical to your smooth functioning as a marketer. Rest of the areas, I am sure your legal person will be hands-on with and will take care of.

Contracts usually go through quite a lot of back and forth with multiple changes before finally getting signed. Please ensure you have copies of all track changes' versions (of MS Word) to be able to trace back if you have missed out on any particular change in this process.

Upon signing off, please keep one copy with yourself, one with the finance department and deposit the original with the corporate legal department.

Once again, I would like to stress upon the fact that as boring as it might sound to you in the first go, but bills and contracts management is going to be a very crucial part of your career. The more unorganized you are, the more time you will spend looking for missed bills, chasing the vendors for bills and chasing the finance team for payments.

Hope you utilize the processes I have explained in this chapter as a marketer, and understand how useful and important these are.

chapter twenty-three

Managing Internal Communications

This is usually a separate department in bigger organizations and sometimes also handled by the HR or the Employee Engagement or the Admin Team depending on the company policies. However, there will always be an involvement of Marketing/Branding Team when it comes to Internal Communications.

Internal Communications is a broad subject on its own, but its basic definition according to me is:

> *Anything that you are communicating with your existing employees, staff or workers using direct messaging or sub-conscious messaging.*

You can be communicating any of the following as part of your internal communications:

1. Vision of the company

2. Mission of the company
3. Company values
4. Company's brand colours
5. Company's yearly/quarterly/monthly targets
6. Company's achievements
7. Employee achievements
8. Employee career growth case studies
9. Internal events communication
10. Special offers from brands or local stores/shops/restaurants/banks, etc. obtained through company tie-ups for employees.
11. Any activity planned at the campus by a brand promoting its products/services at the cafeteria or some other area.
12. Basic manners and etiquette as part of office culture.
13. Women safety and employee awareness over the same.
14. Any deadlines—IT returns filing or PAN card filing, etc.
15. Invitations to board members or senior management or employees for an event or meet.
16. Annual awards and R&R celebration dates and details.
17. Corporate social responsibility messages.
18. Team building activities and other planned exercises for employees.

19. Birthday/anniversary wishes.
20. Newsletters.
21. Corporate magazines.
22. Intranet website for employee engagement and inter-department communication.
23. Any change in the basic policies.
24. Company branded shirts/stationery, etc. for the employees.

I am sure you understand now why I mentioned earlier that usually there is a separate department for internal communications. However, in case you are handling the same for your company, you most likely will need help of your ad agency for most of the above mentioned or otherwise conducted internal communication. You would primarily use either one or many of the following methods to reach out to all the employees:

1. Emailers/E-newsletters

Everything is easy to communicate to your employees by sending an email. Get a nice emailer created by your ad agency with either a form to fill or a hyperlink to click and explore further. The hyperlink can be anything from Google docs to an internal drive depending on where you want employees to go. Emailers should have a catchy subject line and related attractive design.

Since employees are already stressed with work, you should always try to keep the emailer creatives light and funny. Emailers can also have featured employee of the week or a 'Did you know?' section or some other kind of engagement exercise to lighten up and have healthy gossip around it.

2. Newsletter Booklets

This is a more serious type of internal communication done on a quarterly basis usually. Hard copy newsletters are in the form of a booklet with at least 20–30 pages. Content includes MD's message, CEO's message, a cover story, an article by or an interview with one of the senior management personnel, poems or jokes or small write-ups by employees, events and marketing effort in the last three months, any upcoming events, your company in news lately, tips for the season, message from the editor, etc. This booklet is usually distributed to all the stakeholders—employees, board, shareholders, vendors, associates, clients, agencies, potential clients, etc.

3. Branding Elements (internal)

You will generally have various branding elements in your office like standees, LCD screens, meeting room names, various glass walls of meeting rooms and reception area, staff uniforms, office cutlery, direction signage, cafeteria name, cafeteria menu and more. You will need to find out what is the communication you would like to pass on to the employees in their day to day life in the office using these branding elements. Few of them can keep changing based on the latest upcoming event, activity or contest happening in the office. Messages on these elements will be usually generic and not department specific or serious messaging related. These will be lively, fun and engagement driven.

4. Office Interiors

This is the space that will be used by your brand design agency to communicate your brand ethos via use of colours and messaging in the common areas. In employee seating areas, the walls can be used to place images of ideal employees who have done exceptionally well in the organization with their testimonials. This can keep employees motivated since they would generally be looking up to those seniors in terms of growth potential in the firm. You can also have your vision/mission statements and values communicated on the walls. Also, generic quotes from successful people in the industry can be a choice. Same thing with the office cafeteria. You can have some light-hearted, fun messaging on the walls to give it a lively look and communicating that your company cares for its employees. Office interiors work on the subconscious of employees since they notice these more subconsciously during their day-to-day life.

5. Other Collaterals

There are many more collaterals in office spaces forming elements of internal communication like table tops, tent cards in cafeteria, danglers, cut-outs, branded apparels gifted to employees, desktop backgrounds and screensavers, email signatures, event branding, annual calendars and more. These collaterals are used as a supplement to existing internal branding/ communication, on a regular basis to refresh brand engagement with its employees on a seasonal basis.

All the above activities need help of the marketing department and its ad agency in conceptualizing, ideating, designing, copywriting and executing the internal communication required. Hence, either these will be a direct part of your job profile or will come to you indirectly as support towards another concerned department.

Hope this chapter helps you in taking things forward at such times.

chapter twenty-four

What is Social/Business Networking and How to Manage it?

This is one more of my favourite topics. I consider myself as an aggressive networker. Although, networking style completely depends on the place where you are but it can be done at any place, if required.

One of the most basic things that your recruiter or your own company will expect from you as a marketer is to have many ideas in your mind to provide solutions to various problems. And many more contacts who can help you execute the same. Now, this is also a fact that the more people you know and what they do, the more ideas you can give. Meeting more people helps you broaden your mental space towards people and what they are doing for a living. Of course, knowledge gain is another organic result of meeting more and new people regularly. You will find something or other to learn from everyone you meet.

So, don't be shy. As a marketer, people expect you to be a dynamic extrovert who can even have a conversation with a rock. Here are a few things I suggest you do as part of your social/business networking life as a marketer:

1. Join various social/business networking groups

There are various business networking groups and many more social networking groups. You have BNI (Business Networking India), InterNations, Couchsurfing, wine clubs, cigar clubs, rotary club, lions club, various other well-known clubs in your city and many other online groups on LinkedIn, Twitter, Facebook, etc. too. There are many other clubs/groups based on your interest levels like movie clubs, art clubs, pub hopping clubs, singles' clubs, etc. As a marketer, you need to keep on exploring these clubs or groups and understand which of your top 5 choices are suiting your personality, comfort and type of social circle you aspire to be in. Try to be regular and do not miss out various meet-ups happening in these clubs.

2. Always keep your visiting cards with you. ALWAYS!

One of the most important rules of social/business networking is that you should always keep your business card with you. Always! Preferably, in a nice leather visiting card holder or, at least, in your wallet. Generally, the cards kept in a wallet get out of shape and do not look good while exchanging. So, try keeping a visiting card holder or loose ones in one of the pockets of your blazer/coat. Please remember to check before leaving your home or office whether you have enough visiting cards with you or not.

3. Don't be afraid to go out alone

I have come across many people who are either afraid or not interested in going to these get-togethers alone. Their usual question is 'What will I do there alone?' If you are one such fellow, you are not meant for marketing. The art of networking is in reaching somewhere alone and then meet enough people to find the ones you can spend some more time with and have nice conversations or good fun before heading back home. So, always be independent and ready to go out there alone and start networking.

4. Don't be afraid to make the first move

Just like you, most of the others in such social/business get-togethers are afraid to start or strike a conversation with so many strangers around them. But all of them also are as excited as you are to meet many new people. So, the trick to this is that don't spend more than 5–7 minutes at the event without striking a conversation with anyone, it can be anyone who comes across you. This will help you warm up. The longer you will take, the more nervous you might get and push yourself in a corner spending the rest of the evening there without networking at all. So, do the ice-breaking as early as possible. Here's how:

a. First of all, get comfortable with yourself once you enter the venue full of people. Take a few deep breaths, if need be, to bring your heart and mind to a stable level.
b. Be confident of yourself and walk towards the bar or the host of the event.
c. Skim through the whole room while walking and let your instincts help you notice people you find worth knowing before you leave the place.
d. Have a smile on your face ensuring you are comfortable where you are.

e. Order for what you want to drink and in case you have someone standing next to you at the counter, you go… 'Hi, we haven't met.' Extend your hand for a nice firm handshake saying 'I am Xyz…' he will respond to that and that's when you strike a conversation with that person.
f. Never be afraid to go out there and start as many conversations as possible.
g. Do not think of genders while networking. Don't be shy to connect with the opposite gender too.
h. Do not think of nationalities while networking. Talk to all without judging anyone too soon.
i. Don't flirt! Stay focused and do not waste your time doing something that no one is expecting from you.
j. Stay calm.

5. Exchange cards/contact numbers

Another important rule of networking is that you should make sure that you are exchanging your card or contact numbers with the person within the first 60–120 seconds of your interaction. Do not wait for some additional vibes. You are here to network, just exchange cards as soon as possible. An important part to remember after exchanging cards is to not keep it directly in your pocket. Please ensure that you take a look at it on both the sides and make a comment or ask a question about it from the other person. This showcases your genuineness in knowing about the other person and makes them comfortable talking to you further.

6. Don't brag! Listen more

Whatever you are in life, please do not go out there boasting stories about yourself to the people you meet. People always like to be listened. And they like those who listen and are interested in knowing them better. So, please assure yourself that you do not have a point to prove and it will help you if you ask people more about what they do, where they are from and further details as the conversation grows. You will either find that person related to your business or not. In either case, please be polite and interested. In case of your own business, get more details on their requirements, etc. and tell him that you will connect with him later to discuss this in detail and explore working together. Do not start your business pitch then and there. In case of the person being from a completely non-linked area, consider it as your knowledge building time and try and understand his business and work as much as you can in 5 minutes or so.

7. Don't be a pile-on

After basic greetings and conversations specified above, please make sure that you say to the other person 'Alright, it was nice meeting you. I will see you around.' And move on to meet more people. Don't find your solace in one person who talked nicely to you, leaving the rest out. This also happens very often. You meet only a few people and then form groups, more like comfort zones and do not meet the rest of the guests. Please don't do that. Try meeting as many people as you can in the initial hour of reaching the venue. Then you can also start settling in with those whom you found most interesting or friendly.

8. Don't leave too early, nor too late

Please meet all the people you had noticed during your first walk to the bar or while going over to meet the host, before leaving. Have conversations and exchange cards. Do not be in a hurry to leave since your restlessness will not let you stay calm and that will discomfort the people you are getting introduced to. Also, do not be the last one to leave unless you know the host well or you have bonded well during the evening. Stay sober and leave at an appropriate time saying goodbyes to people you met during the event/get-together.

9. Join the after-party, if any and if you are free

Feel free to join any after party being planned by the guests or the host, if you are invited and if you have time for that. This time should be more fun centric than business or work and you can loosen up a bit for it.

10. Communicate next day

Next day, please make sure you drop an SMS (not a Whatsapp or Snapchat message) to all the people you met and exchanged cards/contacts with. You can express how nice it was meeting them and how you would like them to stay connected via LinkedIn or any other respective platform.

11. Online networking next day

Try finding 5–10 minutes next day to search for everyone you met, on LinkedIn or any other respective online platform and send them an invite to connect. This will help you never lose a contact, once made. This also helps you know them better by going through their profiles. If you were not able to find any possibilities of a business association with them earlier, may be going through their profile will help you.

12. Addition to database and mailing list

You should always use MailChimp or any similar tool to stay connected with your network via mails. It is good practice to send at least one mail per month to your list. Content of these mails completely depends on the profession you are in. But you must ensure the content is interesting enough for the people you know and people you have already met. If not using a software and have an office server for SMS/email etc., then you can share the visiting cards to be copied on the server with related details.

13. Schedule a second meeting (if it makes sense)

Few of those whom you will send SMS to will revert and few won't. However, in case you found someone worth meeting one more time in an official manner to explore business opportunities, please feel free to call them and try to fix up a meeting to take things forward. Don't be afraid of the fact that people might not remember you or they might not respond at all. Do your bit and then leave after 2–3 follow-ups.

14. Stay in touch

Whatever the case may be, do try to stay connected with people you know by wishing them on festivals or sending gifts on important occasions or by sharing company calendars or any other corporate gifts. These need not be done with everyone in your contact list but you need to have a well-maintained database in Excel sheet format divided into VVIPs, VIPs and regular contacts. You can reach out to these contacts based on the importance and expenses.

These are few basics I could share with you on social/business networking. Most of the people do not follow it in as much detail as mentioned above, but I can assure you that doing this will help you in the long term.

Happy networking!

chapter twenty-five

Few More Things

Of course, there is much more to marketing than what I could cover in this book. It takes a different shape and level of detailing based on the type of industry as well. I might try to venture deeper into industry-specific advertising and marketing by writing another book.

However, as a marketer you will come across various other terms and activities based on your job profile, budgets in hand and marketing aggressiveness. One such term is 'Brand Capital Deal'.

Brand Capital[1] is part of *The Times of India* Treaty as part of their business development and brand support initiatives. If you have a good budget for your annual

---

[1]http://brandcapital.co.in/

marketing and you are sure of spending a certain value per year on print advertising, you can approach the Times Group to explore Brand Capital Deal. Times Group signs this treaty only with their existing clients sharing long-term relationship. There are few other criteria as well which you can explore as you get serious about the treaty.

The Brand Capital Deal works on the principles of the Times Group coming on board as a partner in your growth. So, you and the representatives from Brand Capital, sit together and analyse your growth in the last few years due to your respective marketing spends. Based on the same and the expected budget for the next 3–5 years, you both decide on the expected sales targets for the coming period of 3–5 years. And, you will also commit on spending an amount on advertisements via various Times Group media vehicles during this period. Generally, the distribution is of 80 per cent amount for print media and the rest for radio, OOH, online, etc. other mediums.

Since you are a Times partner now and have also committed on spending an 'x' amount over a period with details mentioned for each year too, you get the benefit of paying only 'y' per cent of the total Times media cost. This 'y' varies from 70–80 per cent based on the set target expected per year.

Example: If your Brand Capital Deal is based on your 70 per cent target achievement, then if your organization achieves 70 per cent or less of the target mutually decided at the beginning of the contract, you pay only 70 per cent of the total cost of the Times media assets used for your marketing efforts. If you achieve more, you pay the rest of the cost on pro-rata basis. If you achieve beyond 100 per cent of the expected target, then the Times Group would also like to get benefited from the success and this can be decided at the time of the agreement negotiations itself.

Not sure if this will be extremely clear to you in the first read since it is a little more complicated than it looks. However, you can always introduce these options to your company and get benefitted. There are many other such offers by the Times Group and other media houses wherein they come on board as a shareholder partner and help you achieve faster growth and traction.

Medianet/Advertorials is something I could not cover in the print media section. However, this is an extremely important part of your media strategy as a marketer. Few newspaper publications allow you as a marketer to present your brand or products in the form of an article with a copy written like a newspaper article and with pictures either clicked specially for the article via a shoot or provided by you in high resolution format. Of course, they have strict rules regarding the copy, image captions, headlines, etc., which can't be debated with even if you are paying for the medianet/advertorial article. However, this is a good marketing tool to present yourself as more genuine and detailed to your TG as compared to a simple ad. Try using it once. I am sure you will see good results.

Another, upcoming term that you will soon start hearing is **Growth Hacking**. The term has taken various businesses like Dropbox, Pinterest, Instagram, Groupon, and many more to a high growth path in relatively less time. Basically, doing everything it takes to spike your growth without investing much or anything at all in marketing/media plans by being more conscious during product development stages. Also, keep doing A/B testing (testing different versions of the same product to identify the one giving better results of the two) till you reach a perfect product/offer that's so good that everyone will automatically refer it to others. This is a term used in digital marketing but it is going to be the next big thing for sure. So, please get your certification in digital marketing to be able to start using its various aspects and start reading about growth hacking. It will do you good.

In-Film Branding[1] is another area you can use for your brand if it fits well with the situation in a movie and is executed smoothly. There are few agencies that specialize in in-film branding tie-ups and are hired by production houses to crack deals with brands for their presence in various scenes in the movie with room for branding. For example:

Krrish featured brands like Bournvita, Samsung, Lays, etc., *Taal* featured Coke, and *Yaadein* showed Pass Pass, to name a few.

You will get to hear the script used and how your brand will be treated in the scene. You also get to be a part of the shoot for that scene to give your approval. **Brand Association** is another way that you can explore if in-film branding doesn't work for your brand. This is when you connect the theme of the movie or its trailer or a scene with your product and use that part of the film to advertise your product.

Another type of marketing that we did not discuss in earlier chapters is **Cinema Slides and On-Screen Advertising** at various multiplexes or single screen cinemas. Slides are simple static slides placed in front of the projector or played via a PC through projector on

[1]http://www.wsj.com/articles/SB1030630141141036595 and http://www.ripublication.com/gjfm-spl/gjfmv6n1_09.pdf

the screen. On-screen ads are the audio-visual ads that we see on TV as well. This is a wonderful means to catch attention and the best examples are: Manyavar, a men's clothing brand; Byju's, an online learning platform for school students; and several public service announcements. Brands like Manyavar and Byju's have used the cine screen medium wonderfully for some time now to promote their brand to the level where they are at present.

SPECIAL TOPIC 1: Movie Marketing

I thought of categorizing this as a special topic because the philosophy of Movie Marketing is extremely different from the marketing for rest of the products/ services. A movie's fate nowadays is defined by its box office opening weekend. That's it. Hence, it is one of the riskiest investments in terms of returns.

In your usual marketing, you have a longer period to market and correct yourself if required. However, in movie marketing, you do not have any room for correction. It is always a do or die situation.

Another big difference in movie marketing is that we usually set budgets for a year or more for promoting a brand or product, but all marketing budget for a movie is spent within 3–5 months. The marketing is extremely aggressive and apart from basic marketing, PR plays an extremely important role in movie marketing.

For movie marketing, the total budget kept aside is usually 5–10 per cent of the total film budget. And, this budget must be utilized within 3–5 months of the movie release. You will first need to understand your target group for the movie, whether it's for metro cities or for tier-II or III towns or for the masses across the country. Based on the same and the language of your movie, you will target locations for promoting your movie. Based on the locations, you will select media vehicles specific to those regions and accordingly plan a complete marketing strategy.

Before execution, you will look at as many tie-ups and partnerships as possible with various types of media. At the same time your PR stories should start appearing in the Bollywood gossip columns about your movie occasionally. You can work on various in-film branding opportunities and brand associations that can be explored based on the story or cast of the movie.

Before the movie release, the music rights are sold to a music distribution company. Then channel telecast rights are sold to an interested TV channel who wants to be the first to premier the movie on TV. And, then the movie distribution rights are sold to a distributor. All this is done via lot of trade marketing by gaining attention of the trade fraternity. The TV channels come under trade media for movie marketing. Similarly, there are many trade magazines that are read by all the trade fraternity. Using this platform, you market your film within the fraternity and create a buzz to get the most out of music, channel and distribution rights.

There are many more intricate details in movie marketing and all industry specific marketing methodologies and approaches.

◆

SPECIAL TOPIC 2: Marketing as a Career

As a career, I would suggest you don't just look at understanding marketing strategies, planning and execution but also try to understand which industry vertical would you like to make your career in. As you will grow higher up the ladder, the more relevant will your industry experience get. Every industry today is looking for candidates with similar industry experience. So, early in your career, please try to explore 1–2 industries you are attracted to and take a call on sticking with one as soon as you can. This will help you grow faster up the ladder in your career life. With more experience in same field, you understand basics better and hence can focus on advanced strategies for marketing in that industry. You can also devote more time initiating and analysing newer research methodologies and adapting accordingly for better growth of your product/services. Your understanding of competition is higher and you have fixed vendors after being in the industry for a long time. This makes you a 'high returns resource' for the company.

Wherever you are and whatever you are doing, please make sure you do your self-branding and self-marketing. It's important for you to be taken seriously by your colleagues, seniors as well as juniors. Do not shy away from speaking about your achievements (small or big) with your colleagues. Do not miss out on taking credit for something good that you did for the company. Do not delay sharing presentations specifying all marketing efforts as an internal mailer to all the employees every month. Have some numbers supporting your efforts in terms of sales or footfall or leads generated, etc. There is a difference in being modest and being stupid. So, please ensure that your seniors know your efforts well.

I would also recommend you to maintain an Excel sheet with all such efforts listed in the same. This will help you put your contribution in the best possible way at the end of the year during your performance appraisal.

This would be all from my side in this book. If you have any more queries or requests, please feel free to get in touch with me. Thank you for this opportunity to share my knowledge with you.

Acknowledgements

This book has happened due to many people contributing to it and motivating me. As this has been a journey in itself, I would like to thank all those who are associated with this book seeing the light of the day through a story that explains the way it all happened. First of all, my big thanks to all those people, in my personal and professional life, who praised me for my writing skills and insisted that I write a book. But, the aha! moment actually happened during one of the infamous sutta breaks at work when my work friends—Ashish Pandya, Nirmal Debroy and Sameer Manhas asked me to take this seriously and *actually* start writing. Ashish even gave me the confidence that he will help me find a publisher once I am done. That was the moment when I shared with them that I am thinking of writing on marketing and how there are so many things that marketers do at work which are not shared with fresh management graduates, entrepreneurs and junior marketers. They gave a thumbs-up to the idea and the very next day I was writing the first page of this book.

Second part of the discussion happened with my wife Prerana, who loved the idea and supported me by not feeling bad when I spent extra time at home working on the book, after work. Thank you for all your patience and motivation, Prerana. You have always truly stood by my side!

While I was writing this book, I kept on thinking of all the vendors I have worked with during my career as a marketer with various organizations. If it wasn't for them, I wouldn't know the intricacies of the work they do for us marketers. I would like to thank all the vendors I have worked with for fabrication, printing, distribution, gifting, etc. till date. Ad agencies, PR agencies, outdoor media agencies and digital marketing agencies are all elaborated on in the book and, needless to say, my marketing journey would have remained incomplete without their support. I would like to thank all the agencies I have worked with in my career up until now.

As I went on covering one topic after another, the stories of my experiences and incidents with my ex-bosses kept refreshing in my mind. I've come a long way since quitting my job at KPMG and joining Laqshya Outdoor Media, to be a part of the media and marketing industry. I would like to take this opportunity to thank all my seniors and colleagues till date for helping me understand this field better and to push me out of my comfort zone every time I started feeling 'I know it all'. Learning never stops!

Once I completed writing more than half of the book, I started looking for ways to connect with publishers since I was quite new to this field. Many thanks to my friend and well-known writer, Tuhin A. Sinha for introducing me to Kapish Mehra of Rupa Publications. It was the first publishing house I had approached, and Kapish was extremely prompt and professional. Thank you, Kapish and Rupa Publications for showing confidence in me. Your interest in this book made my confidence stronger.

I can't thank you enough, Shambhu, from Rupa Publications, for multiple coordinations that we went through while the book was in production and review. Thank you for being patient and very understanding while I asked you several stupid questions many a times. Many thanks to Tanima from Rupa Publications for pointing out a few updates in the book as well as asking me to write this acknowledgement to show my gratitude to all those who helped me write this book.

I would also like to thank Gaurav Srivastava from *The Times of India*, Pune and Shampa Maitra from Percept Group, Mumbai for helping me out with a few doubts that I had while writing this book. I must also not forget to thank Samier Amritwar of Encyclomedia Global for allowing me to use some images from their work for my chapter on outdoor media.

In the end, I would like to thank all the readers in advance for picking up this book and reading it. I hope you liked it and will write about it on social media to share it with your classmates, friends and colleagues too.

There is a thin line between 'following up' and 'begging'. People on both sides of the table need to understand this. You should neither follow up beyond a respectable limit, nor should you make people follow up with you beyond their respectable limit. When you cross that line by either following up or making people follow up multiple times, you enter the zone known as the 'Unprofessional' zone.

Be careful. Be professional.